SMART COPYRIGHT COMPLIANCE FOR SCHOOLS

A How-To-Do-It Manual®

REBECCA P. BUTLER

HOW TO DO IT MANUALS®

NUMBER 165

NEAL-SCHUMAN PUBLISHERS, INC.
New York   London

Published by Neal-Schuman Publishers, Inc.
100 William St., Suite 2004
New York, NY 10038

Printed and bound in the United States of America.

The paper used in this publication meets the minimum requirements of American
National Standard for Information Sciences—Permanence of Paper for Printed
Library Materials, ANSI Z39.48-1992.

Library of Congress Cataloging-in-Publication Data

Butler, Rebecca P.
  Smart copyright compliance for schools : a how-to-do-it manual / Rebecca P. Butler.
    p. cm. — (How-to-do-it manuals ; no. 165)
  Includes bibliographical references and index.
  ISBN 978-1-55570-646-3 (alk. paper)
  1. Copyright infringement—United States. 2. Fair use (Copyright)—United States.
I. Title.

KF3080.B88 2009
346.7304'82—dc22

2009003621

Dedication

To Tom, who inspired this book.

CONTENTS

LIST OF FIGURES

FIGURES

PREFACE

WHY IS COPYRIGHT COMPLIANCE AND TRAINING IMPORTANT?

Suppose you have gone to several copyright workshops, read journal articles, and even read a few books on copyright in schools. You feel reasonably confident that you understand copyright law and its application in K–12 education. Then one day, you hear that a nearby school has been sued for copyright infringement, specifically computer software violations. You talk to a colleague in that district and learn that they, too, had read some of the same articles and books and had gone to similar workshops. You ask your friend how this lawsuit could have happened, and she says that even though her district had sent some people to copyright training, the district did not have a formal copyright policy or any established process of ensuring that district educators and administrators were in compliance.

You begin to question whether your school could find itself in a similar situation despite the efforts you have made to provide training. When you discuss this question at the next faculty meeting, you learn that the same question was raised at the last meeting of district principals. All involved have the same question: "How can we ensure that our district is in compliance with copyright law so we don't find ourselves in court?"

HOW CAN THIS BOOK HELP?

Smart Copyright Compliance for Schools: A How-To-Do-It Manual evolved from a series of questions and discussion points that have been raised in my copyright classes and in presentations and workshops on copyright that I have conducted over the past 13 years. Time and time again, librarians, teachers, technology coordinators, district administrators, and others have expressed concerns about the schools and districts in which they work—how these organizations do not understand copyright law as it fits into K–12 education or how many of those who work in the organization have little comprehension of what it means to borrow or copy from another's works.

I have come to believe, even when a district has invested in training key personnel and key staff have a good understanding of copyright law, that the school organization and its personnel are often unsure as to how to develop a system that allows them to ensure that they are and remain in compliance with the law. As a result, I determined that a practical manual for educators on how to create a copyright-compliant school was needed.

Unlike my first book, *Copyright for Teachers and Librarians*, this is not a question-and-answer book on how to copy things legally in a K–12 environment. Instead, *Smart Copyright Compliance for Schools* describes to the reader the process by which a school district and/or an individual school (and all of the employees of that district or school) can become and remain copyright compliant. Therefore, this volume addresses the parts of the *process* needed to craft an organization that has accepted the premise that copyright compliancy is to be the norm.

HOW IS THIS BOOK ORGANIZED?

Like my workshops, I have organized this book to feature both how-to steps and practical, real-world examples from a wide range of K–12 schools, both large and small. The first chapter defines what copyright compliancy is and discusses the steps in creating a copyright compliant program. Chapter 2 covers an extremely important part of the compliancy process—the copyright policy itself. In this chapter, readers learn what makes up a strong policy as well as how to write one. Chapter 2 also includes samples from existing school copyright policies.

The third chapter of *Smart Copyright Compliance for Schools* addresses the process, without which copyright compliancy would not exist. It includes the process flowchart. Chapter 4 details copyright procedures, or how those who work in schools implement on a day-to-day basis what is in their copyright policy. It is through these procedures that the copyright policy is carried out. This chapter contains examples of copyright compliancy procedures.

Chapter 5 provides a process for training teachers, librarians, curriculum coordinators, technology specialists, copy center personnel, and others about copyright. Training is essential to ensuring that district personnel understand and can work toward copyright compliancy. Carrying out a thorough training process also evidences that the school makes a good-faith effort to adhere to the law. The sixth chapter illustrates the audit part of the process and includes audit checklist models. Like each of the steps before, auditing is essential for a truly compliant school district. It is the evaluation portion of the process; it indicates how well your district is adhering to your own copyright compliance policy as well as to the law. The final chapter in this book deals with feedback. It is through this step that district/school employees, often identified as stakeholders, are able to see what they are doing right and what needs to be changed or improved. Feedback, coupled with the audit, is the portion of the process that ensures that your district remains compliant.

In addition to the chapters, this book includes seven tools in the "Compliance Toolbox" (located after the chapters and before the index). Tool I: Sample Copyright Compliance Training Materials will be helpful as the organization (school and/or school district) trains its key personnel/stakeholders in copyright compliance. Among the sample copyright compliance training materials included are an initial meeting proposal, a generic training syllabus, and a copyright question-and-answer presentation.

Tool II: Sample Audit Scenario, Audit, and Final Report is composed of three distinct parts: a scenario narrative of a school copyright audit, a model completed copyright compliance audit form, and a sample final report.

Tool III: Sample District Audit Process Annual Planning Calendar and Legend is exactly what the title says: a completed calendar listing when copyright compliance processes will take place and a separate detailed explanation of what these processes are and why they are on the established dates.

Tool IV: Selected Sections of the U.S. Copyright Law covers selected sections of the 1976 U.S. Copyright Law, Public Law 94-553 (Title 17 of the U.S. Code), of importance to those employed in K–12 education, including rights of and provisions for copyright owners; parts of the law of importance to educators, such as fair use and the classroom exemption; and liability limitations relating to online material.

Tool V: School/School District Copyright Policies contains a list of annotated Web sites characteristic of school copyright policies found on the World Wide Web. Their inclusion in this book is not meant to imply that these policies would work in your school district. However, they are examples that illustrate what other schools have chosen to include in their policies. As you write, revise, or re-create your own copyright policy, such examples may prove helpful.

Tool VI: Copyright Teaching and Training Materials on the Internet is also an annotated list of Web sites, this time focusing on copyright instructional materials found on the World Wide Web.

Tool VII: Web-based Copyright Materials (General) is a third annotated list of Web sites. These Internet sites represent a minute selection of the wide variety of material on copyright that is currently available on the Web.

If I have been successful, after reading *Smart Copyright Compliance for Schools: A How-To-Do-It Manual*, you will see that copyright compliance is a relatively straightforward process for establishing a policy, formulating procedures, conducting training and auditing, and providing staff with a process for feedback. With these elements in place and functioning, you will have taken the positive steps necessary to ensure, as well as demonstrate, the intent of your educational organization to be in copyright compliance.

1

INTRODUCTION TO PROACTIVE COPYRIGHT COMPLIANCE

INTRODUCTION[1]

In the 12+ years that I have been teaching copyright to educators, one of the concerns I hear most often is, "I don't want to become the copyright police in my school." The concern is valid. School librarians are often the only educators in the school with copyright training and, by default, are perceived of as the copyright experts. Likewise, the buck stops with the head administrator; ultimately that person is accountable for the school's compliance with policies and laws, including copyright laws and fair use. Along with this, more and more faculty, whether technology coordinators or interested others, are becoming aware of, and sometimes making a study of, copyright as it pertains to them in the school. Additionally, with all these perceptions and interests comes the responsibility of knowing when faculty, colleagues, and students are copying or borrowing materials in an infringing manner and addressing the issue. While an educator may find it easy to correct a student who infringes, correcting a fellow teacher or administrator can be an uncomfortable situation indeed. Therefore, this book focuses on how those interested educators can work together to build whole-school awareness of copyright laws as well as develop working compliance policy and procedures.

Sometimes educators think that being in a nonprofit, educational setting exempts them from complying with copyright laws, especially if they can rationalize that the school or school district has little money and needs the materials. In addition, infringing on copyright law is easy to do. The equipment and supplies needed to copy print, videos, audio, computer software—you name it—are often already in our schools. The ease of duplication on a copy machine, a VCR, a computer, a cell phone, or an iPod often contributes to an educator's cavalier attitude toward the legal implications. So how can the administration, the school library media specialist, and other interested educators work together to create a copyright-compliant school or a copyright-compliant school district?

It is likely that the school librarian or another faculty member, rather than an administrator, will become aware of an infringement. Let's suppose that a school librarian watches a sophomore social studies teacher come into the library, open a sample workbook that a vendor had dropped off in the library a few weeks ago, and line up all 30 students in her class in front of the copy machine. She instructs each student to copy the same activity out of the workbook. When the school librarian approaches the teacher and asks her, in a nonthreatening manner, what she is doing, she answers that there is a great activity in the sample workbook, and the cheapest and quickest way to get it to her class is to have each student make his or her own copy. That way, the teacher reasons, copyright law is not violated.

Section 107 of the copyright law (U.S. Copyright Law, 1976), the section covering fair use, *does* say that within the parameters of the purpose and character, nature, amount and substantiality, and the effect of the use on the potential market, copies of items can be made for educational purposes. However, the teacher continues, "This workbook is so great! I am going to have my class make individual copies of each activity in the workbook—one each week for the whole semester—that way we don't have to spend the money for each student to get the workbook; we get to use all of these great activities and we are not infringing on anyone's copyright!"

The librarian knows that a workbook is a consumable. While it may be acceptable to copy one activity from the workbook for a one-time immediate need, to reproduce multiple copies of the whole book over the course of the semester could be considered an infringing use, one reason being that it represents a financial loss to the publisher. At this point the library media specialist faces a dilemma. How is he or she going to convey copyright information to the teacher without offending her? No matter how nonjudgmental this is stated, the teacher may interpret this to mean that the librarian does not have the best interests of the school and students at heart.

COPYRIGHT COMPLIANCE DEFINED

Copyright compliance is the choice of an organization to comply with copyright law. For the purposes of this book, this can be interpreted as school districts (and the district's individual schools) choosing to work within federal copyright law to borrow from and copy works in a legal manner. This choice will normally be formalized with the creation of a district copyright compliance policy.

SCHOOL DISTRICTS AND COPYRIGHT COMPLIANCE—PAST AND PRESENT

Because copyright law in the United States is based originally on English common law (Butler, 2004), some semblance of the concept of owning one's creative works (and following the established laws of the land) has been part of our collective mind-set since before we became a nation. This includes in educational environments, such as the K–12 school. Indeed, we find mention of educators and copyright ranging from the time of Noah Webster (Butler, 2004), to that of audiovisual materials of the late 1950s (Reed, 1958), to that of the 21st century (Hoffmann, 2001; Crews, 2006). Overall, books, print and Web articles, and other materials created and published for educators seem to take the stance that everyone be legal, even as many teachers, librarians, school administrators, and others verbalize that they should not need to follow the law, because "education does not have enough funds" (ETT 542T, 2007). So is it *really* important to be copyright compliant?

IMPORTANCE IN THE 21ST CENTURY

Copyright is affected by a strange confluence of law and ethics. It is indeed law (U.S. Copyright Office, 2008). It is also an ethical concern. Enforced by the Federal Bureau of Investigation (FBI) (U.S. Copyright Office, 2007), working within the arena of copyright law seldom finds us with FBI agents lurking over our shoulders.[2] Therefore, one could argue that we are actually enforcing ourselves. Thus the moral dilemma: if it is possible that no one will know we are borrowing/copying without permission or a license, is it okay to do so? In reality, of course, this is no different from any other situation we may find ourselves in where we know something is illegal or wrong but we also know that we probably won't get caught should we decide to do it. For example, we inadvertently run into another car in a parking lot and cause what we know to be hundreds of dollars' worth of damage to that car. We look around and see that no one else saw what happened. Do we leave our name and insurance information or just drive off? The same holds true for copyright law: owners of copyrighted works have a right to profit from their ownership; to take from these individuals or groups without permission is a moral as well as legal issue. The bottom line is that just because we can get away with something doesn't make it right. Now let's look to what is involved in the conception of a copyright compliance plan.

STEPS IN THE CREATION OF A PROACTIVE COPYRIGHT COMPLIANCE PROGRAM

The following eight steps are key in the creation of a proactive copyright compliance program[3] (see also Figure 1.1):

- Establish and communicate a district copyright compliance policy.
- Establish and communicate the copyright compliance procedures.
- Analyze organizational impact.
- Determine copyright training needs.
- Provide necessary copyright training.
- Audit the copyright process for compliance.
- Provide feedback for copyright process improvement.
- Maintain copyright compliance.

ESTABLISHING AND COMMUNICATING THE COPYRIGHT POLICY

The school district first needs a copyright policy. It is possible that the district already has one. If this is the case, then the policy needs to be read and studied by those setting up the compliance process in order to establish that said policy complies with copyright law. If there is no policy, or if it does not work in light of copyright compliance, then a new/revised policy needs to be developed. Additionally, to be fully successful, the district's copyright compliance policy needs to be communicated to the shareholders, that is, the school board, administrators, faculty, staff, and students. People cannot comply with a policy they do not know exists. (Policy issues are discussed in Chapters 2 and 3.)

ESTABLISHING AND COMMUNICATING COPYRIGHT COMPLIANCE PROCEDURES

The procedures that enforce the copyright policy are also important. Once again, the district may already have copyright procedures. If not, such practices either need to be developed and/or revised to meet the new policy.

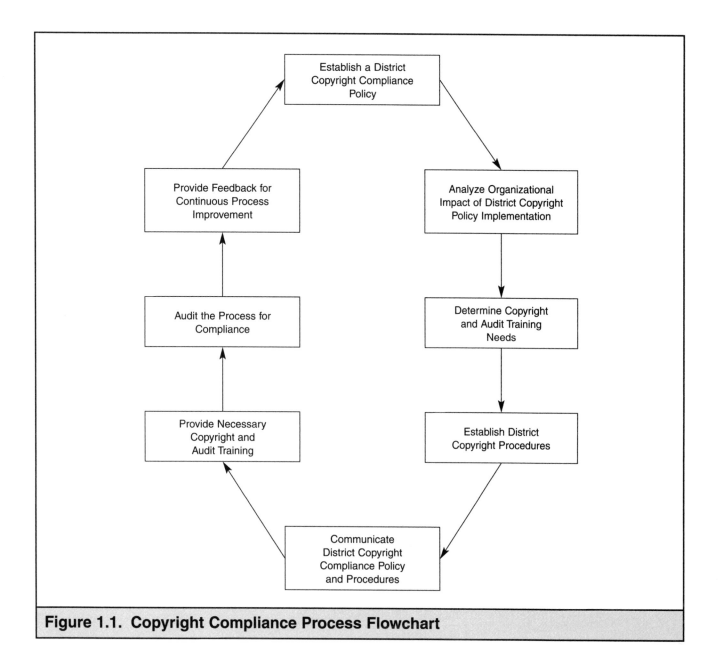

Figure 1.1. Copyright Compliance Process Flowchart

The procedures and their presentation to the shareholders are covered in Chapters 3 and 4.

ANALYZING ORGANIZATIONAL IMPACT

The third step in the creation of a proactive copyright compliance program is to study how the policy and procedures will affect the district, the individual school communities, and the shareholders within the district (school librarians, administrators, technology coordinators, teachers, etc.). Analysis of organizational impact will be done during the initial meetings (Chapter 3). Clearly, compliance with copyright law and the district policy requires initial and ongoing work by district employees. Questions to ask in terms of the organizational impact include:

- Who will be involved in developing the policy?
- Who will need to be trained?
- Who will do the training?
- Who will be our internal experts?
- Who will be our auditors?

While answers to these questions may not be known when you begin the compliance process, it is important to realize that there will be an impact on job responsibilities and that this needs to be kept in mind as the process is established.

DETERMINING COPYRIGHT TRAINING NEEDS

Another instrumental step in the process is to establish how shareholders are trained in proactive copyright compliance. In the compliance process, this training includes:

- Training the appropriate people how to comply with copyright law
- Informing the shareholders of all information contained in the copyright policy
- Preparing those who will serve as process auditors

This step is also determined during the various meetings discussed in Chapter 3.

PROVIDING COPYRIGHT TRAINING

Who is trained? What aspects of copyright compliance are needed? Who does the training? These questions are answered in Chapter 5. Additionally, Tool I in the "Compliance Toolbox" provides sample copyright compliance training materials.

AUDITING THE COPYRIGHT PROCESS FOR COMPLIANCE

Once the policies and procedures as well as organizational impact and training have been determined and presented, the entire course of action needs to be evaluated; in other words, is the proactive copyright compliance process doing what it sets out to do? This is the purpose of the auditing process. Process auditing information can be found in Chapter 6, Tool II, and Tool III.

PROVIDING FEEDBACK FOR IMPROVEMENT

Chapter 7 discusses who is responsible for feedback and what should be done with it. The purpose of including a method for providing feedback is to ensure that the district's policy remains current. In addition, this allows for continuous improvement of the compliance policies and procedures.

MAINTAINING COPYRIGHT COMPLIANCE

Last, this book concludes with how copyright compliance can be maintained in the school district. Maintenance of the process is part of the purpose of auditing. This is covered in Chapters 6 and 7 of this book. Additionally, flowcharts in several of the book chapters illustrate each of the copyright compliance steps (see Figure 1.1), and Tool IV in the "Compliance Toolbox" at the end of this book provides excerpts from U.S. copyright law.

CONCLUSION

Let's go back to the story in our introduction. Remember the high school librarian who observed a sophomore social studies teacher with the unique idea for a way to get around copyright law? What happens now?

Frankly, at this point, it may be too late for a positive outcome. Without whole-school awareness of copyright laws and the guarantee of support from the school administration *before* a violation occurs, this school librarian might decide to ignore the copyright infringement. If the librarian confronts the teacher, the teacher may become angry or defensive. If the school librarian turns to the administration, the librarian may feel more like he or she has tattled rather than attempted to instill ethical behavior. In any case, faculty relationships are damaged and legal compliance is at risk. It is this sort of thing that we hope to avoid with district-wide and school copyright compliance. Chapter 2 looks at the establishment of a district copyright compliance policy.

NOTES

1. Please note: Chapter 1 is partially based on the following article: Butler, Rebecca P. 2008. "Join the Copyright Compliance Team." *Knowledge Quest* 36, no. 3 (January/February): 66–68.
2. "Seldom" does not mean "never." It is certainly possible to receive a "cease and desist letter," be part of copyright litigation, or receive a fine for violating copyright law—even in the K–12 school environment (Torrans, 2003: 44–45).
3. Please note that this list of steps does not exactly match the copyright compliance flowchart. The list is composed of elements of the copyright compliance process that have been combined for ease of discussion in this chapter. The flowchart, however, is the process itself, in the order in which the program elements should occur.

REFERENCES

Butler, Rebecca P. 2004. *Copyright for Teachers and Librarians*. New York: Neal-Schuman Publishers.

Butler, Rebecca P. 2008. "Join the Copyright Compliance Team." *Knowledge Quest* 36, no. 3 (January/February): 66–68.

Crews, Kenneth D. 2006. *Copyright Law for Librarians and Educators: Creative Strategies and Practical Solutions*, Second Edition. Chicago, IL: American Library Association.

ETT 542T Class Discussion. 2007 (July 24). DeKalb, IL: Northern Illinois University.

Hoffmann, Gretchen McCord. 2001. *Copyright in Cyberspace: Questions and Answers for Librarians*. New York: Neal-Schuman Publishers.

Reed, Paul C. 1958. "Editorial: Archives and Copyrights." Reprinted from *Educational Screen & Audio-Visual Guide* (May): 1.

Torrans, Lee Ann. 2003. *Law for K–12 Libraries and Librarians*. Westport, CT: Libraries Unlimited.

U.S. Copyright Law. 1976. Title 17, sections 107 and 108.

U.S. Copyright Office. 2007. "Stopping Copyright Infringement." Available: www.copyright.gov/help/faq/faq-infringement.html (accessed April 23, 2008).

U.S. Copyright Office. 2008. Homepage. Available: www.copyright.gov/ (accessed April 22, 2008).

2 THE COPYRIGHT POLICY

INTRODUCTION

Let's assume that you are in a school district with no copyright policy, one that has not been updated in many years, or one that appears incomplete (for example, containing only copyright guidelines and no parts of or quotations from the actual law). Is what you have enough, given your wish to develop and maintain a copyright compliant district complete with all copyright compliant schools? Or should you update, change what you have, or write a new policy?

The focus of this chapter is on the school district copyright policy. Here we define, detail, and discuss the policy contents as well as cover how to write and communicate a copyright policy. Figure 2.1 shows the copyright compliance process flowchart, with the first step in the process, "Establish a district copyright compliance policy," highlighted. (Please note that the fifth step, "Communicate district copyright compliance policy and procedures," is also highlighted. This step is addressed later in this chapter as it connects to the copyright policy.)

SCHOOL DISTRICT COPYRIGHT POLICY: DEFINITION AND AUDIENCE

According to the *Merriam-Webster Online Dictionary* (2008), a policy is "a definite course or method of action selected from among alternatives and in light of given conditions to guide and determine present and future decisions." A school copyright policy, then, is established and accepted by a particular school district and outlines how it will comply with copyright law in its day-to-day operations.

The audience of the school district/school copyright policy can vary from district to district. However, the most common audience is comprised of the stakeholders: librarians, technology specialists/coordinators, teachers, administrators, the school copy center director, and other school district employees. With some policies, the district's students are also addressed,

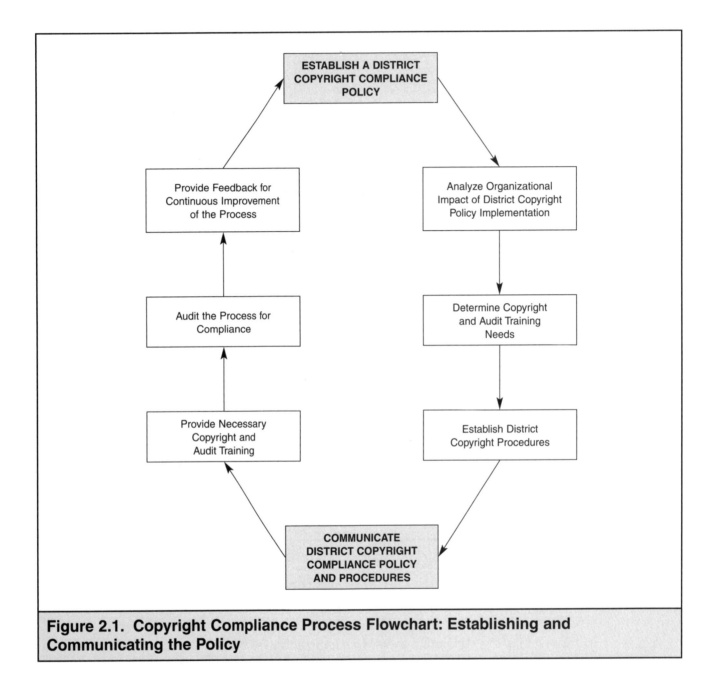

Figure 2.1. Copyright Compliance Process Flowchart: Establishing and Communicating the Policy

although it is more likely that student use will be inferred in the main policy and the students find a short copyright statement in the school acceptable use policy ("Almance-Burlington School System Copyright Guidelines," 2006; "Bellingham School District 501 Board Policy," 1995; Chicago Public Schools, 2003; Columbus Ohio City School District, n.d.).

Within the policy audience, there are normally two types of readers—those who skim the policy and those who read it thoroughly. The "skimmers" are usually busy people. In order for them to retain the main informational points, the points need to be (1) toward the beginning of the policy, (2) at the start or end of the paragraphs, and (3) highlighted (Kellough, 2007). Thorough readers are often skeptical, believing that what is written could be incorrect. They will (1) give the policy a "close" (careful) reading, (2) dispute author's claims, and (3) question the validity of the document. In order to convey information to the "skeptic," it is crucial to support all points with documentation, citations, and details (Kellough, 2007). Both of these types of readers will be in almost any audience that reads the school district copyright policy. Therefore, it is important to keep such readers in mind as we turn to what is contained in a district-wide copyright policy.

CONTENTS OF A DISTRICT-WIDE COPYRIGHT POLICY

Surf the World Wide Web and you will see myriad copyright policies. Many are for schools and/or school districts, specifically addressing school district employees or existing as a part of a student acceptable use policy. Other copyright policies are designed for academic, commercial, and medical environments. It seems as though organizations throughout the world have need of a copyright policy. As you look over these policies, you may come to the realization that copyright issues really do exist in all of these environments, and although the venues may not be the same, what the law says often is.

Now notice that some of the policies are quite long, covering many pages and formats of materials, and some are very short, saying only that the organization in question should "follow the law." You will also observe that some policies contain direct quotes from the copyright law, while others seem to include only copyright guidelines. (Some good points to remember about copyright law and guidelines are: Copyright law is federal law, updated periodically by acts passed by the U.S. House and Senate. Congress also creates copyright guidelines; however, they are not law. Instead, guidelines are nonbinding statements that help us to abide by the law. By following guidelines, users are considered to have acted in good faith; that is, they tried to follow the law to the best of their abilities. Copyright guidelines represent the least amount that a user can borrow from the owner of a work [Butler, 2004, 2008]. Statutory exemptions, or parts of the copyright law, often afford the user more than the minimum that he or she can borrow or copy.) Thus, whether you are planning on writing a new policy or updating or revising an old one, looking at other policies to see what is included and/or excluded can be informative. (Tool V: School/School District Copyright Policies gives a number of URLs to access for examples of copyright policies.) What, then, are the contents of a "good" copyright policy?

Much as the interpretation of copyright law and guidelines can depend on who is doing the interpreting, where and how the work is being copied, and the format of the work, so, too, can the contents of the copyright policy reflect these various items. Additionally, some districts and schools stick to the law, others borrow liberally from guidelines, and still others use a combination approach. Furthermore, some school districts ascribe to the notion that the shorter policy is superior, while others feel that the more information, the better. Thus, school district copyright policies can range from one paragraph to 30 or more pages ("Duplication of Copyrighted Material," 1997; "Copyright Implementation Manual," 2002; Roggow, 2007; "A Quick Reference Employee Copyright Handbook," 2003). As a result, there are probably no "perfect" policies that can be recommended for a specific school district or school; however, many policies may work wholly or in part. Those sections most often found in a school/district copyright policy are the introduction, pertinent pieces of the law and/or guidelines, presentation of fair use (either the statutory exemption, which is part of the actual law, and/or the guidelines), discussion of how the various formats (print, video, audio, computer software, Internet, etc.) can be used within the law/guidelines, and more.

Next we outline and discuss the types of regulations that are usually found in a school copyright policy. Remember, if there are items specific to your school or district that belong in such a policy that are not included in the following sections, then add these items to those more common points featured in this chapter.

SAMPLE CONTENT OUTLINE—SHORT COPYRIGHT POLICY

The short copyright policy is basically a general statement informing readers that the school district intends to follow copyright law or the guidelines and that, as employees, they are also to do so. There may additionally be a sentence or two in the short policy in terms of widespread copying and/or permissions. The following is an example of a short policy statement: "Duplication of copyrighted material will be in accordance with law. Administrative approval is required whenever duplication of extensive portions of a copyrighted material is proposed for class usage" ("Duplication of Copyrighted Material," 1997: 5). Another example of a short policy statement is: "libraries will adhere to copyright guidelines and procedures as outlined in *The Copyright Primer for Librarians and Educators* (Bruewelheide, 1995). Each school library maintains a current copy of this booklet" ("Administrative Policies," 2002: 8).

SAMPLE CONTENT OUTLINE—LONG COPYRIGHT POLICY

Lengthy copyright policies often include parts of the copyright law and/or guidelines, which the policy author(s) instruct the district/school employees to follow. Points frequently found in bigger documents are outlined here.

   I. Introduction
  II. Definitions
 III. Statutory Exemptions or Guidelines for Copying/Borrowing
      Works
      A. Fair use
      B. Format of works and related statutory exemptions and/or
         guidelines for each
         1. Print
            a. Books
            b. Periodicals
            c. Other formats
            d. Single copies
            e. Multiple copies (for use in the classroom)
         2. Visual media
            a. DVDs
            b. CDs
            c. Videos
            d. Off-air recordings
         3. Music
            a. Audio media (in any format)
            b. Sheet music
         4. Digital media
            a. Internet
            b. Computer software
            c. Databases
            d. Multimedia
  IV. Permissions
      A. How to request permission
      B. Sample permission form
   V. Copying Limitations
      A. Infringement examples
      B. Consequences of illegal copying
      C. Infringement reporting within the district
         1. How
         2. To whom
  VI. Compliance Procedures (see Chapter 4)
 VII. URLs and Print Sources to Reference for More Informational
      Support

Next the various parts of this long (generic) copyright policy are discussed. After each section is a sample of what that part of the policy might
look like. Examples have been taken either from existing school district
copyright policies or created by the author of this book. One of the purposes of this book is to provide examples of working documents. These
may or may not succeed in your particular educational environment. Just
as with copyright law, the choices of what belongs in your copyright policy

should be those of the stakeholders, that is, the individuals who know the school district and schools best and understand what is needed.

Introduction

The beginning of a school district/school copyright policy usually includes some sort of introduction. This introduction might address those for whom the policy is written; cover why the district/school has a copyright policy, give a general statement about respecting copyright law and the rights of intellectual property owners, make a statement that district employees are not to violate copyright law at any time or for any reason (this sort of statement could also be located in the "copying limitations" section of the policy), request that all those who wish to copy use a specific permission request form (provided by the school/district), and/or state that the district will not be responsible for any copyright infringements made by its employees ("Almance-Burlington School System Copyright Guidelines," 2006; "Bellingham School District 501 Board Policy," 1995; Levine, 2000). Remember that copyright law and copyright guidelines are both open to the interpretation of the users/borrowers (and owners) of works. This can sometimes make the interpretation of a copyright policy difficult. As a result, some school/school district copyright policies also have a statement in or near their introduction (such a statement could additionally be located at the end of the policy) that says something to the effect that the school/district is not giving legal advice, only recommendations ("Copyright Guidelines: A Manual for Canby School District Employees," 2003; "Copyright Guidelines for Okaloosa County Public Schools," n.d.). So, let's look at what belongs in the body of the policy.

Definitions

Definitions are included in school/district copyright policies when those writing the policy feel that explanations for terms used in said policy are needed. Sample terms to define include *copyright, electronic mail, Internet, brevity, archival copy, fair use, home use only,* and *public performance* (Chicago Public Schools, 2003; "Copyright Guideline Handbook," 1999; "Copyright Manual and Materials Selection Guide," 2001).

Statutory Exemptions or Guidelines for Copying/Borrowing Works

This section of the school/district copyright policy is typically the longest. Here the reader finds information on fair use in addition to other statutory exemptions (parts of the law) or guidelines concerning the formats of works that can be copied.

Sample Introduction

District _____ believes in respecting the rights and property of all individuals. All district employees are to adhere to the law, guidelines, and procedures provided in this policy in order to comply with the U.S. federal copyright code. District _____ is not liable for copyright infringements that result from the actions of its employees.

Sample Definition

Public performance is defined as a performance in a place open to the public or at any place where a substantial number of persons outside of a normal circle of a family and its social acquaintances is gathered. Schools have special privileges when it comes to performing copyrighted material in public. Section 110(1) states that "performance or display of a work by instructors or pupils in the course of face-to-face teaching activities of a nonprofit educational institution, in a classroom or similar place devoted to instruction . . . [is not an infringement]." This material presented must be related to the lesson plan in order for these exemptions to apply.

Source: "Copyright Manual and Materials Selection Guide" (2001).

Fair Use as Law and Guidelines

Fair use is written into U.S. federal copyright law. It limits the rights of the copyright owner. In other words, fair use lets users borrow from owners' works without obtaining permission or a license from the owners or their representatives or without needing to find a work in the public domain. Remember, *public domain* is the term used to define works that anyone can copy or distribute as much of and as often as they want. For example, most federal government documents[1] are in the public domain ("Copyright Law of the United States and Related Laws Contained in Title 17 of the United States Code," 2007). Fair use is composed of four basic factors. The first is the purpose and character of the use—*why* the work is being used. This is the point that educators often migrate to since copying works for educational use is more acceptable, under this part of the law, than is using such works for a commercial venture. The second fair use factor is the nature of the work—is the work fact or fiction, published or unpublished? Basically, factual and published pieces work best here. The third fair use factor is how much of the work in question is being borrowed or copied. This fair use factor is measured both quantitatively—number of words, length of the movie, number of frames in the musical score—and qualitatively—borrowing the "heart" of the work is borrowing too much. The fourth and final fair use factor is concerned with the marketability of the work under consideration. What this means is, if the user borrowing part or all of the work causes the work's owner to lose money or the ability to sell his or her work, then the borrowing should not take place (Butler, 2004). There are also fair use *guidelines*. As we covered earlier in this chapter, guidelines are not law, although Congress may approve them. Basically, this means that the borrower of a work will probably never receive a cease and desist letter (a letter sent by owners or their attorneys when works are being used without permission) or be named in a copyright lawsuit, as long as he or she follows the guidelines under which borrowing from a particular work fits. Many school districts find using copyright guidelines easier than trying to interpret copyright law. This is because guidelines[2] give exact numbers, while the law requires deciphering what the user *thinks* is the explanation. However, guidelines are much more restrictive than the law, thus the dilemma for many educators. In most school/district copyright policies, fair use is covered somewhat early on, either as the law, as guidelines, or both ("Copyright Condensed," 1999; Copyright Basics and Guidelines, n.d.; "Copyright Laws," 1995; Roggow, 2007).

Next, we turn to types of works and the laws and exemptions that explain their use, copying, and borrowing.

Sample Statutory Exemption: Fair Use

4.2 Section 107 of the Copyright Act, "Limitations on Exclusive Rights: Fair Use" (Full Text)

Notwithstanding the provisions of sections 106 and 106A, the fair use of a copyrighted work, including such use by reproduction in copies or phonorecords or by any other means specified by that section, for purposes such as criticism, comment, news reporting, teaching (including multiple copies for classroom use), scholarship, or research, is not an infringement of copyright. *In determining whether the use made of a work in any particular case is a fair use the factors to be considered shall include:*

1. the *purpose* and character of the use, including whether such use is of a commercial nature or is for nonprofit educational purposes;
2. the *nature* of the copyrighted work;
3. the *amount* and substantiality of the portion used in relation to the copyrighted work as a whole; and
4. the *effect* of the use upon the potential market for or value of the copyrighted work. The fact that a work is unpublished shall not itself bar a finding of fair use if such finding is made upon consideration of all the above factors.

Source: 4.2 of Section 107 of the U.S. Copyright Act. Taken from the Groton Public Schools "Copyright Implementation Manual" (2002: 11).

Formats of Works and the Law and/or Exemptions

In many district copyright policies there is an extensive area that focuses on several of the more common formats that works may take and the law and/or exemptions that fit with copying these works. For example, there will be a section on print. This section will focus on the copying/borrowing of material from books, periodicals, newspapers, and other print sources. In this area, there is also usually discussion on the differences within the law and/or guidelines between making a personal copy and making multiple classroom copies. The personal versus multiple copies also is covered with most other media discussed in this section: visual (digital and analog) media such as DVDs, CDs, videos, and off-air recordings such as television programs; music in all formats (CDs, off-air recordings, sheet music, etc.); and digital media, such as the Internet, computer software, databases, and multimedia created using a variety of digital sources ("Copyright Basics and Guidelines," n.d.; "Copyright Guidelines: A Manual for Canby School District Employees," 2003; "Watertown Unified School District Copyright Policy," n.d.).

Sample Guideline

MULTIPLE COPYING [The format under discussion is print.]

Multiple copies (one copy per pupil in a course) can be made if it meets the criteria of brevity, spontaneity, and cumulative effect, and if each copy contains a notice of copyright.

1. *Brevity*—A complete poem printed on no more than two pages or an excerpt from a longer poem not to exceed 250 words copied in either case. A complete article, story, or essay of less than 2,500 words or an excerpt from prose less than 1,000 words or 10 percent of the work, whichever is less, but in either event a minimum of 500 words to be copied. One chart, graph, diagram, drawing, cartoon, or picture per book or periodical issue.

2. *Spontaneity*—Copying is done by the teacher when there is not a reasonable length of time to request and receive permission to copy.

3. *Cumulative Effect*—The copying is only for one course and only nine instances of multiple copying per course during one class term is allowed. Not more than one short poem, article, story, essay, or two excerpts may be copied from the same author, nor more than three from the same collective work or periodical volume during one class term.

Source: "Copyright Laws" (1995: 12.2).

Permissions

This is a common section to many copyright policies. It often includes instructions on the permission process as well as a sample permission form. The sample permission form is sometimes included in one of the appendices ("Copyright Guideline Handbook," 1999; "Copyright Guidelines: A Manual for Canby School District Employees," 2003; "A Quick

Sample Permission Letter Instructions

1. If this request is to copy copyrighted materials, state the

   - number of copies;
   - type of reprint (e.g., photocopy)
   - type of distribution (e.g., in-class handout, coursepack);
   - type of use (e.g., supplementary teaching materials, in-class presentation); and
   - duration of use (e.g., current school term, multiyear).

2. If this request is to perform/display copyrighted materials, state the

   - type of performance/display;
   - number of performances/displays;
   - anticipated date range of performance/display; and
   - anticipated audience for the work.

3. If this request is to incorporate copyrighted materials into a multimedia or online work, state the

   - nature of the work into which the materials are to be incorporated;
   - types and dates of performance or publication of the work (including Web posting); and
   - anticipated audience for the work.

4. For all of the above, supply the required information and a completed sample letter form (see page 19 of this handbook) to your immediate supervisor/division chair and then to the Director of Curriculum and Instruction.

5. The Director of Curriculum and Instruction will then prepare and send an official request ("Copyright Guideline Handbook," 1999: 18).

Reference Employee Copyright Handbook," 2003; "Bellingham School District 501 Board Policy," 1995).

Copying Limitations

Another area found in various school district copyright policies is that on the limitations involved in copying. This category may include examples of how school district employees might infringe on another's ownership—for example, what school district employees can and cannot copy, the consequences (either federally or in the school district) of illegal copying, and how infringements are reported within the districts (and to whom they are reported) ("Bellingham School District 501 Board

Sample Copying Limitations #1

[This sample pertains to software only.]

Teacher users *can*:
(Teacher users are any certified teacher in a self-contained or specialized classroom.)

- Check out single-user or lab pack licensed software for classroom use only providing that its installation is within the restrictions listed on the software.

Teacher users *cannot*:

- Make archival or home use copies of any software.
- Copy any software for illegal distribution and/or sale.
- Install any school-owned software for home use.
- Download programs from the Internet without the direct permission of the principal and/or technology coordinator.

Source: "Software Copyright Policy" (2002: 3–4).

Sample Copying Limitations #2

COPYRIGHT INFRINGEMENT BY DISTRICT EMPLOYEES

A. Consequences of Infringement

    1. No Indemnification. Under Section 895.46 of the Wisconsin Statutes, District employees who violate federal copyright laws may be deemed to have acted outside the scope of their employment and may not be eligible for any indemnification or legal counsel otherwise provided by the District.

    2. Penalties. District employees who infringe copyrights may be personally liable for copyright infringement. Under Sections 502 through 506 of the Act, the penalties for infringing a copyright include becoming subject to an injunction to stop the infringement, payment of actual damages suffered by the copyright owner, disgorgement of any profits made by the infringer resulting from the infringement, an assessment of statutory damages, payment of costs and attorneys' fees, impoundment of copies during the pendency of an infringement suit, and destruction of copies as part of the court's final judgment.

Source: "Watertown Unified School District Copyright Policy" (n.d.: 15).

Sample Copying Limitations #3

Infringement—violation of copyright law

- Protected by federal law, can result in civil action (fines) and can be a felony.

Source: "Copyright Basics and Guidelines" (n.d.: 1).

Policy," 1995; "Eden Prairie Schools," 2000; Hart et al., 1996; "Software Copyright Policy," 2002).

Compliance Procedures

District and/or school copyright compliance procedures (and examples) are discussed in Chapter 4 of this book.

URLs and Print Sources to Reference for More Informational Support

There are millions of Web sites dealing with copyright and schools,[3] covering policies, procedures, law, guidelines, copyright forms, quizzes, help sites, and more. Thus, some school/district copyright policies contain a listing of places on the World Wide Web where more information might be obtained ("Copyright Guidelines: A Manual for Canby School District Employees," 2003; "Copyright Guidelines for Okaloosa County Public Schools," n.d.; "Copyright Implementation Manual," 2002; "Copyright Guidelines: A Manual for Lane Education Service District," 2000). (See Tools V, VI, and VII in the "Compliance Toolbox" for a sample list of copyright Web sites.)

ADDITIONAL (OPTIONAL) SECTIONS

Some of the larger school/district copyright policies may additionally include sections such as the following.

How to Officially Register a Work with the U.S. Copyright Office

Although it is somewhat rare to find this section in a copyright policy, when there, this section usually gives contact information for the U.S. Copyright Office and general directions for how to officially register a work.

How a Work Is Copied

In most copyright policies, the copying of materials by scanner or another particular copying device is considered just copying and is not addressed separately. However, once in a while, there is a policy that addresses how something is copied.

Frequently Asked Questions

Often this section is located in an area focusing on copyright procedures rather than in the body of the copyright policy. Once again, however, one may find a policy with sample questions and concerns in it.

Photocopying for Library Reserve or Other Reasons

Once again, *why* the photocopying is done is not usually addressed in the copyright policy. However, it is broken out at times. The assumption is that it was of importance to the policy author(s).

Sample Copyright Registration Information

To register your work [with the U.S. Copyright Office], you will need to do the following:

1. Obtain the necessary forms.
2. Complete the appropriate application.
3. Send a nonrefundable filing fee.
4. Attach 1 or 2 non-refundable copies of the work.

Source: Butler, *Copyright for Teachers and Librarians* (2004: 10).

Sample Information for Copying a Work

Scanners

- Using a computer scanner to convert print material into digital form is a violation of copyright laws unless it meets the fair use copyright guidelines or permission is granted from the author.

Source: "Copyright Guidelines for Okaloosa County Public Schools" (n.d.: 1).

Sample of Frequently Asked Questions

5. A teacher has a program recorded off the air and it fits the curriculum so well the teacher wants to keep it for use again next year. Can this be done?

After a 45-day period, all off-air recordings must be erased or destroyed immediately.[4] The teacher's other options are to write for permission to retain the program or to inquire into purchasing it.

10. A teacher sends a student with music to be copied for rehearsal purposes because the music has been forgotten at home. Is this legal?

No, music may be copied only in an emergency for performance. Teachers should not direct students to request illegal copies.

Source: "Copyright Policy and Procedures" (1995: 14–15).

Sample of Why Copying May Be Done

PHOTOCOPY FOR LIBRARY RESERVE USE

At the request of a teacher, a librarian may photocopy and place on reserve excerpts from copyrighted works in its collection in accordance with *fair use* guidelines....

Source: "Copyright Manual and Materials Selection Guide" (2001: 13).

Copy Center Information and Form

While not all K–12 schools or school districts have their own copy centers, those that do may be mentioned in the district copyright policy. Usually there is a short directive as to the responsibilities of the copy center, often followed by a sample copy request form. Please note that copy center personnel and users must abide by the same copyright law, copyright policies, etc., as the rest of school district personnel.

Sample Copy Center Directive

> The primary purpose of the Copy Center is to provide copies of materials to schools and departments at a minimal cost. The Copy Center attempts to return as many jobs as possible the morning following receipt of job requests. Completion of all jobs is not always possible within the normal workday.... All jobs received in the Copy Center will be completed according to due date. Please allow ample time for the completion of jobs. (School District of South Milwaukee, 2007: 1)

Sample Copy Request Form

Types of items on a copy request form include name, department, and contact information for person requesting the copying; date of request; date copies are needed by requestor; account and/or budget numbers; what needs to be copied and how many times; and special requests, such as color of paper, collated or not, etc. A good suggestion (see Figure 2.2) is to add a copyright compliance statement such as "The _____ School District adheres to copyright law and the school district copyright policy" to the copy request form.

Historical Bibliography

This is found only seldom in a copyright policy. It appears that the author(s) may want to remind the policy readers/stakeholders that copyright in the K–12 school has been around for many decades.

Sample Historical Bibliography

Steinhilber, August W. *Copyright Law: A Guide for Public Schools.* Alexandria, VA: National School Boards Association, 1986.
Vicek, Charles. "Writing Your Own School Copyright Policy." *Media and Methods* 24, no. 4 (1988): 27–29.
Video and the Copyright Dilemma. Luling, LA: St. Charles Parish Public Schools, n.d.

Source: "Copyright Manual and Materials Selection Guide" (2001: 34).

COPY CENTER
Thomas Jefferson High School
District 1234
Thomas Jefferson, Illinois
Phone: 123-123-1234
Email: CC@TJHS.edu

Requestor Name: _____   Date of Request: _____

Department: _____   Delivery Location: _____

Phone Number: _____   School Account Number: _____

E-mail: _____   Date Copying Needed By: _____

Item to Be Copied: _____   Number of Copies Needed: _____

Special Requests: _____

The Copy Center of Thomas Jefferson High School adheres, at all times, to the U.S. Copyright Law and the District 1234 copyright policy.

Figure 2.2. Sample Copy Request Form

Sample Plagiarism Guideline

3. If students use an author's ideas, they must give the author credit, either in text or in a footnote. If they use an author's words verbatim, the words must be put in quotation marks or there should be other indications of a direct quotation. Failure to give credit to an author is plagiarism.

Source: "A Quick Reference Employee Copyright Handbook" (2003: 29).

Plagiarism Guidelines

Plagiarism, "using others' ideas and words without clearly acknowledging the source of that information" ("Plagiarism," 2004) is *not* copyright. However, because both it and copyright have in common that another person's works are used without permission, some authors will include a plagiarism statement or set of guidelines in the district copyright policy (this statement is usually addressed to the district's students). It is not necessary to do so and may confuse the readers/stakeholders into thinking that these two terms are one and the same ("Copyright Condensed," 1999; "Copyright Guidelines for Okaloosa County Public Schools," n.d.; "A Quick Reference Employee Copyright Handbook," 2003; "Copyright Manual and Materials Selection Guide," 2001).

Copyright Notices

Again, this is one of the notifications that one would expect could come under "copyright procedures." However, a few school districts include sample copyright notices in the copyright policies.

Signature Line

A few policies require that district/school employees sign that they have read and understood the copyright policy.

Sample Copyright Notices

[This sample notice is for placement near a photocopying machine.]

NOTICE
The copyright law of the United States (Title 17, U.S. Code) governs the making of photocopies or other reproduction of copyrighted materials. The person using this equipment is liable for any infringement.

Sample Signature Line

I, _____, agree to follow the copyright policy of _____ School District.

Signed:

_____

Dated: _____

Appendices

Not all school district and/or school copyright policies contain appendices. However, where found, appendices contain information that the policy author(s) believe is important but is not found in the body of the policy. Examples of appendices might be a brief explanation of the Digital Millennium Copyright Act (DMCA) or a summary of the Technology, Education, and Copyright Harmonization (TEACH) Act (Roggow, 2007). The appendices might also include samples of forms used in copyright compliance—for example, a "copyright questionable use notice," which notifies district infringers (and their administrators) that they may be in violation of copyright law (Simpson, 1999), or a permission form.

WHAT A DISTRICT COPYRIGHT POLICY IS NOT

The district copyright policy is not a school or library materials' selection policy, although sometimes a copyright policy is embedded within a selection policy. It is also not an acceptable use policy (AUP), which addresses

---

Sample Appendix

Permission Letter

<Your address and date>

<Name and address of copyright owner/publisher>

To Whom It May Concern:

I am a librarian at _____ School. I am writing to ask for your permission to copy [bibliographic data: title, author (if available), copyright date, distributor/publisher, place of publication] for placement on a school Web page. This Web page, which will be available to the public for [amount of time/dates], supports our student homework hotline.

If you are willing to grant permission, could you sign and date below? I have provided [an SASE or Web address] for your response. Moreover, if there is someone whom I should be contacting instead of you, could you provide me with the name and address of this person/group?

Thank you for your time in this matter.

Sincerely,

<Your name>

PERMISSION GRANTED TO _____ School to use my work for placement on their homework hotline Web site for [amount of time/dates].

Copyright holder's signature _____ Date _____

Source: Butler, *Copyright for Teachers and Librarians* (2004); "Copyright Guidelines: A Manual for Lane Education Service District" (2000).

things such as privacy, commercial advertising, and unauthorized access to resources in addition to a copyright statement. Examples of copyright statements found in AUPs include the Columbus, Ohio, "Student Acceptable Use Regulation," which contains a short copyright infringement statement in the same area as the plagiarism infringement statement. The copyright statement is as follows:

> You will respect the rights of copyright owners. Copyright infringement occurs when you inappropriately reproduce work that is protected by a copyright. If a work contains language that specifies appropriate use of that work, you should follow the expressed requirements. If you are unsure whether or not you can use a work, you should request permission from the copyright owner. Copyright law can be very confusing. If you have questions, ask a teacher. (Columbus Ohio City School District, n.d.: 3–4)

Another copyright statement example is from the Naperville (Illinois) Community Unit School District 203 student "Authorization for Internet Access." It is as follows:

> Some examples of unacceptable uses are: a. Using the network for any illegal activity, including violation of copyright or other contracts, or transmitting any material in violation of any U.S. or State regulation; b. Unless authorized by a District Official, downloading of software, regardless of whether it is copyrighted or de-virused; and c. Downloading copyright material for other than personal use. (Naperville Community Unit School District 203, n.d.: 1)

The Chicago Public Schools also include some copyright concerns within their "Student Acceptable Use of the CPS Network." These include, under the "unacceptable uses" section: "1. Use of the CPS Network for, or in support of, any illegal purposes" (Chicago Public Schools, 2003: 3) and "9. Using copyright materials, including commercial software, without permission of the copyright holder, and in violation of state, federal or international copyright laws" (Chicago Public Schools, 2003: 4). Thus, although AUPs may have a short copyright statement within them, they do not have the many other points normally seen in a school copyright policy, such as specific laws and guidelines, permission statements, and so on. Furthermore, copy center work orders, although they may address the law or some of the copyright guidelines as part of the total document, are not policies. A school copy center work order normally includes such things as (1) who is asking for the work done, (2) the date submitted, (3) the date needed, (4) the number of copies required, (5) how the copies are to be printed or copied (for nonprint items), and (6) any special instructions.

Next we turn to how to maintain an up-to-date policy.

ENSURING THE POLICY IS CURRENT

Copyright law is constantly evolving. This is mainly because technology formats are changing so rapidly that the law cannot keep up. As a result, at any one time in Congress there are a number of bills covering various aspects of copyright in House or Senate committees and subcommittees waiting to be introduced, discussed, or voted on (American Library Association, 2008). What this all means is that it can be quite difficult to be current in what is happening with copyright law. However, such currency is very important when working toward copyright compliance. So, what does the school district/school do to keep the copyright policy "state of the art?" First of all, there needs to be a procedure in place to review the district copyright policy periodically. (See Chapter 4 for more information on such a procedure.) Next, how can these groups keep up-to-date in school issues and copyright law?

One way to maintain copyright currency in the K–12 educational environment is through professional organizations. Specialized groups such as the American Library Association (ALA), American Association for School Librarians, Association for Educational Communications and Technology (AECT), American Association of School Administrators, National Association of Elementary School Principals, National Association of Secondary School Principals, Urban Superintendent's Association of America, and more can help school employees maintain copyright currency through conferences and presentations, committee meetings (both the ALA and AECT, for instance, have copyright or intellectual property committees), and blogs, listservs, wikis, and other professional online communication tools. In addition, many professional organizations publish specialized journals with columns and articles covering copyright and other ethical concerns. For example, there is a social responsibility column in *Knowledge Quest* (AASL professional journal) and a column titled "Copyright and You" in *TechTrends* (AECT professional journal) that focus on copyright law in school environments. Other journals written for specific educational professionals, such as *School Library Journal*, also maintain copyright columns. There are as well, at any one time, a number of books dealing with copyright law and schools that can be consulted for more information (Bruwelheide, 1995; Butler, 2004; Crews, 2005; Hoffmann, 2005; Lipinski, 2006, 2009; Minow and Lipinski, 2003; Russell, 2004; Simpson, 2005; Torrans, 2003). (See Tools V, VI, and VII in the "Compliance Toolbox" for listings of copyright articles, Web sites, etc., that are informative in providing the latest in terms of copyright law.) Additionally, there are a multitude of URLs covering copyright law, guidelines, issues, policies, etc. And, of course, the U.S. Copyright Office maintains a comprehensive Web site covering copyright law at www.copyright.gov.

Next we discuss how to write a copyright policy.

HOW TO WRITE A COPYRIGHT POLICY

WORKING WITH AN EXISTING COPYRIGHT POLICY

Sometimes it is difficult to find an existing copyright policy. It may be so old that you are hesitant to continue using it; it may be hidden in the superintendent's office or in a library drawer. Sometimes it makes sense to the reader; other times it is a confusing jumble of law, guidelines, and "common sense," as interpreted by the original author. Once again, what do we do? Do we assume that we need to write an entire new policy, or what?

If there is already a policy available, the copyright policy committee should read it over carefully. They then need to discuss it: does it contain what is needed for copyright compliance? If not, what is missing? (See the section on copyright policy content at the beginning of this chapter for information on what is needed.) The committee can elect to rewrite the policy, add to it, or keep it as it is.

WRITING A NEW COPYRIGHT POLICY

There is no one specific way to write a copyright policy. However, there are a number of things that appear commonplace to any such project. Two are (1) convene a group (or find an individual) who appears to be able to start and complete such a project and (2) study what other schools have already done (see also Tool V—policies from other schools/school districts can give you content direction as to what looks appropriate and what makes you and your fellow stakeholders uncomfortable). Other items important to writing a copyright policy include (3) find and refer to information from a wide variety of educational and copyright sources, such as professional organizational information, copyright material on the Web and in books, etc.; (4) use professionals, such as copyright lawyers or other copyright experts; and (5) make certain that the total document is written in an understandable manner, that is, it is both inclusive and succinct ("IT Professions and Lockergnome," 2007; University of California–Berkeley, n.d.; University of Minnesota, 2005).

Who Writes the Policy?

Those who write and/or revise the copyright policy can vary from district to district. However, it is important that those who work on the policy are knowledgeable in copyright law and its application within the school environment. Writing and revising a policy is often best as a collective effort—for example, a committee composed of a number of school/school district individuals with "buy-in" and some knowledge of copyright law. The groups that might provide representation to such a committee include school administrators, librarians, technology specialists, and teachers. Additionally, a member of the school board might be on the committee and/or a school attorney. While the committee can be composed of representative individuals, it should not be so large as to be unwieldy. You need to go with what works best in your district, such as five to six people. In some cases, a subgroup, perhaps of school librarians who have taken a copyright class, might write up a working policy. This is then presented to the main committee for review, discussion, and revisions. Eventually the final policy is submitted to the school board (and, depending on your district, the school administration) for approval.

POLICY COMMUNICATION AND TRAINING

The school district copyright policy should be communicated to all employees verbally, as a part of the formal meetings at the start of each school year as well as a part of all new employee orientations (see Chapter 3). Additionally, the policy should be available in print at key locations in each of the schools and in the district offices, including but not limited to: all main administration offices (superintendent(s) and principals), all libraries, all technology centers and computer labs, on main bulletin boards, and near all copy machines. The policy should also be accessible online, in an easily reached location, on the school Web page.

All district employees should receive copyright policy training at least annually or whenever the policy is changed. Such training can be done by an internal expert (someone within the district who has received adequate copyright law training and who is familiar with the district copyright policy) or by an external expert who is a copyright authority and has reviewed and/or approved the district policy. (Policy training is described in depth in Chapters 3 and 5.)

CONCLUSION

In this chapter we have discussed the following parameters of the copyright policy:

- What is in it
- What the copyright policy is not
- How to write the policy
- How to ensure that it remains current
- Who writes it
- How to work within an existing policy
- How to communicate the policy
- When policy training is done
- Who does the training

Your policy is now ready, and you know who will train the school employees and when. Now it is time to look to the copyright compliance process as a whole. Chapter 3 covers the experts, both external and internal, and the meetings needed to establish, develop, and evaluate a district (and school) copyright compliance process.

NOTES

1. While most federal documents, including the U.S. Constitution, the Declaration of Independence, and many other government publications, are in the public domain, once in a great while the federal government will decide to publish something of which a work's author/owner wishes to retain ownership. In such a case, the document is *not* in the public domain. Therefore before copying, do check the copyright notice to see who owns a work.
2. A popular set of guidelines used in many schools/districts is Hall Davidson's two page "Copyright and Fair Use Guidelines for Teachers" (n.d.) found under "Copyright Resources" on his download page www .halldavidson.net/downloads.html#anchor923173 (Davidson, 2008).
3. A Google search found 112,000,000 hits for "copyright and schools" (Google, 2008).
4. This sample of frequently asked questions illustrates part of the copyright *guidelines* for off-air recordings.

REFERENCES

"Administrative Policies." 2002. East Moline, IL: East Moline School District 37.

"Almance-Burlington School System Copyright Guidelines." 2006. Available: www.abss.k12.nc.us/modules/cms/pages.phtml?sessionid= 2b02ed4198fd7b593b1c0b4383d799ab&pageid=2677&sessionid= 2b02ed4198fd7b593b1c0b4383d799ab (accessed August 1, 2008).

American Library Association. 2008. "Copyright Legislative Agenda." Chicago: American Library Association. Available: www.ala.org/ ala/washoff/woissues/copyrightb/federallegislation/ copyrightagenda/ cpylegagenda.cfm (accessed July 22, 2008).

"Bellingham School District 501 Board Policy 2314: Copyright Compliance." 1995. Available: www.bham.wednet.edu/technology/ techpolicies.htm (accessed August 1, 2008).

Bruewelheide, Janis. 1995. *The Copyright Primer for Librarians and Educators*. Chicago: American Library Association.

Butler, Rebecca P. 2004. *Copyright for Teachers and Librarians*. New York: Neal-Schuman.

Butler, Rebecca P. 2008. *Practical Copyright for Illinois School and Public Librarians*. (Presentation/PowerPoint). Peoria, IL: Illinois Institute for School and Public Librarians.

Chicago Public Schools. 2003. *Chicago Public Schools Policy Manual: Student Acceptable Use of the CPS Network*. Chicago: Chicago Public Schools.

Columbus Ohio City School District. n.d. "Student Acceptable Use Regulation." Available: www.columbus.k12.oh.us/staup_revised.pdf (accessed August 1, 2008).

"Copyright Basics and Guidelines." n.d. Mooseheart, IL: Mooseheart School.

"Copyright Condensed." 1999. Johnston, IA: Heartland Area Education Agency 11.

"Copyright and Fair Use Guidelines for Teachers." (n.d.) Available: www.techlearning.com/ (accessed August 11, 2008).

"Copyright Guideline Handbook." 1999. LaGrange, IL: Lyons Township High School District 204.

"Copyright Guidelines: A Manual for Canby School District Employees." 2003. Available: www.trulia.com/school-district/OR-Clackamas_ County/Canby_School_District_86/ (accessed August 1, 2008).

"Copyright Guidelines: A Manual for Lane Education Service District." 2000. Eugene, OR: Lane ESD.

"Copyright Guidelines for Okaloosa County Public Schools." n.d. Available: www.okaloosa.k12.fl.us/technology/standards/teacher/ copyinfo.htm (accessed August 1, 2008).

"Copyright Implementation Manual." 2002. Mystic, CT: Groton Public Schools.

"Copyright Law of the United States and Related Laws Contained in Title 17 of the United States Code." 2007. Available: www.copyright .gov/title17/ (accessed August 1, 2008).

"Copyright Laws." 1995. Plainfield, IL: Plainfield School District.

"Copyright Manual and Materials Selection Guide." 2001. Lake Charles, LA: Calcasieu Parish Public School System.

"Copyright Policy and Procedures." 1995. Hopkins, MN: Hopkins School District 270.

Crews, Kenneth. 2005. *Copyright Law for Librarians and Educators: Creative Strategies and Practical Solutions*. Chicago: American Library Association.

Davidson, Hall. 2008. "Copyright Resources." Available: www.halldavidson.net/downloads.html#anchor923173 (accessed August 3, 2008).

"Duplication of Copyrighted Material." 1997. Arlington Heights, IL: Arlington Heights School District 214.

"Eden Prairie Schools: Media." 2000. Eden Prairie, MN: EP Schools.

Google. 2008. s.v. "Copyright and Schools." Available: www.google .com/search?q=copyright+and+schools&ie=utf-8&oe=utf-8&aq= t&rls=org.mozilla:en-US:official&client=firefox-a (accessed October 15, 2008).

Hart, Mary, et al. 1996. *Copyright: Multimedia and a Whole Lot More*. Indianapolis, IN: Association for Educational Communications and Technology.

Hoffmann, Gretchen. 2005. *Copyright in Cyberspace 2: Questions and Answers for Librarians*. New York: Neal-Schuman.

"IT Professions and Lockergnome." 2007. Available: www.lockergnome .com/it/2007/11/16/best~practices-for-policy-writers/ (accessed August 1, 2008).

Kellough, Victoria. 2007. "Tailoring Employment Documents for a Specific Audience." West Lafayette, IN: The Writing Lab and The OWL, Purdue University. Available: owl.english.purdue.edu/ owl/resource/638/01/.

Levine, Elliott. 2000. "A Policy on Paper Could Save Your Web Site." *School Administrator* 57 (November). Available: www.aasa.org/ publications/saarticledetail.cfm?ItemNumber=4182.

Lipinski, Tomas A. 2006. *The Complete Copyright Liability Handbook for Librarians and Educators*. New York: Neal-Schuman.

Lipinski, Tomas A. 2009. *The Librarian's Legal Companion*. New York: Neal-Schuman.

Merriam-Webster Online Dictionary. 2008. s.v. "Policy." Available: www .merriam-webster.com/dictionary/policy (accessed July 17, 2008).

Minow, Mary and Tomas Lipinski. 2003. *The Library's Legal Answer Book*. Chicago: American Library Association.

Naperville Community Unit School District 203. n.d. *Authorization for Internet Access*. Naperville, IL: Naperville Community Unit School District 203.

"Plagiarism: What It Is and How to Recognize and Avoid It." 2004. Bloomington, IN: Indiana University. Available: www.indiana.edu/ ~wts/pamphlets/plagiarism.shtml (accessed August 2, 2008).

"A Quick Reference Employee Copyright Handbook." 2003. Rosemount, MN: Independent School District 196.

Roggow, Judith (Ed.). 2007. "School Copyright Policy and Guidelines." Minneapolis, MN: DeLaSalle High School.

Russell, Carrie. 2004. *Complete Copyright: An Everyday Guide for Librarians*. Chicago: American Library Association.

School District of South Milwaukee. 2007. "Copy Center." South Milwaukee, WI: School District of South Milwaukee.

Simpson, Carol. 1999. "Managing Copyright in Schools." *Knowledge Quest* 28, no. 1: 18–22.

Simpson, Carol Mann. 2005. *Copyright for Schools: A Practical Guide*. Columbus, OH: Linworth Publishing.

"Software Copyright Policy." 2002. Chicago, IL: Medill Elementary School.

Torrans, Lee Ann. 2003. *Law for K–12 Libraries and Librarians*. Westport, CT: Greenwood Publishing.

University of California–Berkeley. n.d. "How to Write a UC–Berkeley Campus-wide Policy." Available: http://campuspol.chance.berkeley .edu/HowtoWriteACampuswidePolicy.pdf (accessed August 1, 2008).

University of Minnesota. 2005. "Guide to Writing University Policy." Available: www.fpd.finop.umn.edu/groups/ppd/documents/ information/guide-to-writing.cfm (accessed August 1, 2008).

"Watertown Unified School District Copyright Policy." n.d. Watertown, WI: Watertown Unified School District. Available: www.watertown .k12.wi.us/pages/wsud_copyright.cfm (accessed August 9, 2008).

3

THE PROCESS

INTRODUCTION

It was determined in Chapter 1 that there are eight steps in the copyright compliance process: establishing and communicating a district copyright compliance policy, establishing and communicating the copyright compliance procedures, analyzing organizational impact, determining copyright training needs, providing necessary copyright training, auditing the copyright process for compliance, providing feedback for copyright process improvement, and maintaining copyright compliance. In order to complete these steps, we start with those who first conceptualize the need for district and/or school copyright compliance. Such people could be any concerned individuals/groups: school superintendents, principals, school media specialists, technology coordinators, teachers, the school board, and/or members of the community.

Let's imagine that a district school superintendent watches as another district loses a lawsuit involving the illegal copying of software onto classroom computers. The district superintendent decides she wants to ensure that a similar situation is unlikely to ever happen in her district. How does she start the process of copyright compliance? Well, once the need has been determined, it is essential that she, as the first stakeholder, find those who would help her achieve her goal—the experts.

EXPERTS

Two types of experts can help a school district or school become copyright compliant: the outside experts and those internal to the school community itself.

OUTSIDE EXPERTS

Who might the outside experts be? Given the goal of copyright compliance, these could include intellectual property[1] lawyers, preferably those focusing on copyright law; a college or university academic who teaches, researches, and writes in the area of copyright, such as a technology, education, or law professor; a qualified representative of a professional copyright organization[2]; or a copyright expert from an association that promotes the ethical and legal use of materials, such as the American Library Association (ALA), the American Association of School Librarians (AASL), or the Association for Educational Communications and Technology (AECT). Using outside experts may require some research on the stakeholders' parts and include a fee.

Outside experts can be used to do the following:

- Coordinate the entire copyright compliance process.
- Train the trainers (the internal personnel who will then advise or train all other district/school employees).
- Review and approve the district copyright policy, create a new one, or revise an existing policy.
- Conduct the compliance audits.
- Serve as an online service provider agent.
- Act as the district "go-to" person.

INTERNAL EXPERTS

Internal experts are those already in your school district or school who have knowledge and interest in copyright as it pertains to the school environment and/or knowledge and interest in process auditing procedures. Such individuals may include school librarians, technology coordinators, curriculum leaders, and administrators, many of whom have had training in copyright law as a part of their undergraduate and graduate college and/or university experiences. These people can also be used in a similar manner to what is described previously for the outside experts. For example, internal experts can do the following:

- Coordinate the entire copyright compliance process.
- Train the trainers.
- Review and work with the administration and school board to approve the district copyright policy, create a new one, or revise an existing policy.
- Conduct the compliance audits.
- Serve as an online service provider agent.
- Act as the district or school "go-to" person.

Additionally, internal experts can, as part of their teaching and administrative work, model ethical and legal copyright behavior and teach students about copyright law.

The flowchart (see Figure 3.1) demonstrates how to determine whether the district "go-to" person should be an external or internal expert. The

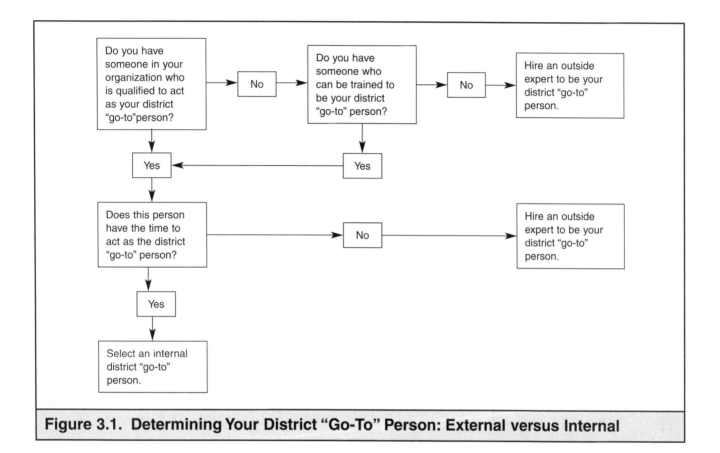

Figure 3.1. Determining Your District "Go-To" Person: External versus Internal

sidebar, corresponding to the flowchart, discusses each decision point in detail.

THE DISTRICT AND/OR SCHOOL "GO-TO" PERSON

Whether external or internal, the designated "go-to" person in a district or school needs to be very familiar with both copyright law and the district policy. Keep in mind, should this individual be an outside expert, that the school district still bears the responsibility for copyright compliance. The "go-to" person is necessary, because copyright questions and issues will arise. As such, it is important to have someone in the district and/or school whom all other employees can contact in order to obtain answers about copyright law and the district/school policy. It is also important to establish a "go-to" person to ensure that copyright issues/questions are addressed consistently across the district/school. An external "go-to" person may be placed on retainer by the district or school. An internal "go-to" person may be someone at the district office or a knowledgeable person from one of the schools (for example, a high school library media specialist who has taken courses in copyright law and education).

The flowchart for selecting your school or district "go-to" person has several decision points. The following briefly describes each decision point and its importance:

Decision 1: Do you have someone in your organization who is qualified to act as your district "go-to" person? A qualified internal person would be someone who is current in copyright law as it applies to the schools in your district. This person must also be capable of and committed to remaining current in the law as it changes. In addition, the

(cont'd.)

person should be someone who is a good communicator and who wants to act in the capacity of "go-to" person.

Decision 2: Do you have someone who could be trained to be your district "go-to" person? This person should be someone who is good working with external policies, procedures, laws, etc. It would also be helpful if the person's job is related to copyright law in some way.

Decision 3: Does this internal person have the time to act as the school or district "go-to" person? In all likelihood, the person you have in mind for the "go-to" person already has a full schedule. It is important to realize that this position will require time above and beyond the person's normal job duties. Depending on the size of your school and/or district, this time commitment could be substantial. In some instances, the "go-to" person will be required to research copyright questions as issues arise, and this research could be time-consuming.

If the three decision points are determined to be "no," then turn to an external expert/"go-to" person.

No matter who the "go-to" person is, it is important to communicate to all school district employees the identity of this person and how to contact him or her. It is also important to ensure that all copyright questions asked of the "go-to" individual are routed through a common source so that there is consistency in the application of both the law and the policy. For example, an administrative assistant might be charged with the collection of copyright questions from all school employees. He or she would then turn them over to the "go-to" person, who would respond to each question in a timely fashion. Either the administrative assistant or "go-to" person could also be in charge of collecting all reported examples of copyright infringement that occur within the district or school. These could then be brought to the administration or school board for discussion and possible action. An online service provider (OSP) agent would be involved in all online copyright infringements. Please see discussion of online service provider agents in the following section.

ONLINE SERVICE PROVIDER AGENTS

The OSP agent is the person designated by the school or district to receive all reports of online copyright infringement. He or she may also be the "go-to" person for the organization. According to the U.S. Copyright Office (2008),

> The Digital Millennium Copyright Act, signed into law on October 28, 1998, amended the United States Copyright Act, Title 17 of the U.S. Code, to provide in part certain limitations on the liability of online service providers (OSPs) for copyright infringement. Subsection 512(c) of the Copyright Act provides limitations on service provider liability for storage, at the direction of a user, of copyrighted material residing on a system or network controlled or operated by or for the service provider, if, among other things, the service provider has designated an agent to receive notifications of claimed infringement by providing contact information to the Copyright Office and by posting such information on the service provider's publicly accessible website.

What this means is that any school or district that acts as an online service provider[3] needs to designate someone as the person (agent) to whom all online copyright infringements are reported. The online service provider agent is (1) to be listed in the "Directory of Service Provider Agents for Notification of Claims of Infringement," found on the U.S. Copyright Office Web site; (2) to report all online copyright infringements via the identified school/district to the U.S. Copyright Office; and (3) post all reported infringements on a school Web page available to the public. If the school/district does so, then their liability concerning copyright violations that occur via their online service is lessened from what it would be without such a designated agent. (See "512. Limitations on liability relating to material online" in Tool IV in the "Compliance Toolkit.")

It is imperative that the district and/or school "go-to" person and/or online service provider agent be trained by an expert in copyright law, as it applies to the school educational environment, before taking such a position. This person would also need to be instructed in the specifics of the district copyright policy, perhaps by one who was involved in the writing of the policy. Once identified, this "go-to" person/OSP agent would additionally want to be kept current in both copyright issues and district policy issues, receiving refresher training in both at least biannually or whenever major revisions to the law or policy occurred. Furthermore, this individual should be required to maintain access to a copyright expert (perhaps the external trainer) and a district policy expert in order to have support for those questions that he or she could not answer in either area. Ideally, the district "go-to" person could also facilitate a team of internal school "go-to" people who would meet periodically to ensure consistency in the application of both copyright law and the district copyright compliance policy. Please note, it is very important to communicate the identity of the school copyright "go-to" person to all employees at the school so that they know who to contact when copyright expertise is needed.

The next piece of this chapter speaks to the meetings involved in becoming a copyright compliant district and/or school. However, before these meetings are addressed, it is imperative to first consider the school district copyright policy. If the district has such a policy, it should be reviewed for currency prior to the initial meeting described in the following section. If such a policy does *not* exist, then it must be established prior to the initial meeting (see Chapter 2).

So our district superintendent, presented in the introduction, now has an idea of *who* her experts are to be. What is next?

MEETINGS

Next on the agenda are the meetings, which first set up and then continue the copyright compliance process.

INITIAL MEETING

The purpose of the initial meeting is to meet with the initial and perceived stakeholders in order to propose a process to ensure copyright compliance and analyze the organizational impact in which such a process will result. Discussion at this meeting includes input from district participants (those identified as internal participants previously) and focuses on the process and how it will affect the organization (school district and/or school) and the initiatives required to implement the process. It is at this point that an external expert is helpful. Such an impartial outside person can facilitate the meeting in a nonbiased manner—and obtain feedback from meeting participants—more effectively than could an internal person. This is because an external person may be less likely to have any real or perceived agenda in the process.

Items that the meeting leader might provide for this first meeting include proposed processes, in the form of narratives and flowcharts, which contain the organizational impact and role of the stakeholders in implementing the copyright compliance process, sample training materials and illustrative activities, sample auditing materials, and proposed follow-up activities. (The different items described in this paragraph are discussed in later chapters.)

Estimated length of time for this first meeting would be about two hours, the first hour for the introductory materials and the process discussion and the second hour for a basic copyright question and answer session. Given the nature of the subject area, questions dealing with copyright will tend to crop up at various times. While the purpose of this first meeting is not as an informative session on copyright law, it is helpful to let participants begin expressing their copyright concerns at this time.

Things to do at this first meeting include determining whom the policy developers, trainers, experts, and auditors will be, and whom will be trained. It is important that all initial meeting participants understand that there will be an impact on the job responsibilities of many within the organization as a result of the copyright compliance process.

Outline of the Introductory Meeting

The following is an outline of the types of topics that need to be discussed at the initial meeting.

    I. The Main Question
       A. What does a school district, serious about copyright law, need to have in place in order to be copyright compliant?
    II. What Is Needed
       A. Copyright policy
          1. What should be in it?
             a. Are all the bases covered?
             b. Who will check to make sure it is followed?
          2. Who will communicate the policy?
             a. District staff
             b. School administrators
             c. Library media specialists

       d. Copy center director

       e. Individual school faculty and staff

    3. How will it be communicated?

       a. Teachers' meetings

       b. Web page

       c. Binders

B. Procedures for copyright compliance

    1. Establish the copyright compliance policy

    2. Establish copyright compliance procedures

    3. Communicate the policy

    4. Provide necessary training and documentation

    5. Audit the process

    6. Provide feedback

C. Formal copyright training

    1. Who will be trained?

       a. Teachers

       b. Librarians

       c. Technology coordinators

       d. Copy center personnel

       e. Students

       f. Others

    2. Who will train?

       a. District level personnel

       b. Administrators

       c. Librarians and technology coordinators

       d. Others?

    3. What will be trained?

       a. Copyright compliance for K–12 schools

    4. How will the training occur?

       a. Outside resources (and possibly trainers)

       b. Internal trainers

D. Formal copyright auditing

    1. What is the process?

       a. To document compliance

       b. To show good intentions

       c. To help ensure continuous improvement

    2. Who will audit?

       a. Outside auditors

       b. Internal auditors

       c. Combination?

    3. How will we audit?

       a. Surveys

       b. Focus groups

       c. Other?

    4. When will we audit?

       a. Continuously?

        b. Annually?

        c. Once per semester?

   E. Training materials

      1. World Wide Web

      2. Books

      3. Articles

      4. Copyright classes and workshops

      5. Selected resources' handouts

      6. Other?

   F. Feedback

      1. How?

        a. Documentation

      2. When?

        a. End of year?

        b. Continuously?

 III. Basic Copyright Q&A Session

Examples of What Might Be Generated by the Participants at the First Meeting

The following are samples of what might be generated by the first meeting participants. These items are bulleted below, with possible answers (which will depend on your initial meeting and the discussion it generates) beneath each bulleted suggestion.

- Who communicates the policy and procedures?
  - School board
  - Administration
  - Outside expert
  - Other

- How are the policy and procedures communicated?
  - Teacher in-services
  - New teacher meetings
  - Need-to-know basis
  - When there are copyright issues/problems/trouble

- To whom are the policy and procedures communicated?
  - Administration
  - Faculty
  - Staff
  - Activity sponsors
  - Parents
  - Interested others

- Who will audit the copyright compliance process?
  - The outside expert
  - An internal expert from the administration

- ○ The internal expert/"go-to" person
- ○ Other
- • When will auditing occur?
  - ○ Whenever there is the need, "trouble"
  - ○ Once a semester
  - ○ Once a year
- • Who is accountable for what?
  - ○ Probably will not be determined at the first meeting
- • Copyright questions

Do not be alarmed if a few of these first meeting participants are less than excited about some or all of the processes being generated. Such individuals, whether librarians, technology specialists, teachers, or others, might feel that the school administration is "forcing" them to be at the meeting; feel that they already "know" everything being discussed and presented; or feel threatened (perhaps because they realize that they, themselves, may be infringing on others' copyrights). In such a circumstance, it is best to continue the meeting as planned. You cannot control what others think, feel, or their agenda, only your own, and that is to achieve a copyright-compliant district or school.

FOLLOW-UP MEETING(S)

Following the initial meeting, follow-up meetings to iron out the details of the items identified previously will almost certainly be required. These follow-up meetings may include everyone who attended the initial meeting; however, it would probably be more efficient and effective to break the initial group into subgroups of the initial meeting participants and assign specific tasks. The follow-up meetings will include procedures meetings to establish compliance procedures, training meetings to establish training requirements, and audit meetings to establish audit procedures.

If the follow-up meetings are conducted in subgroups, a final follow-up meeting of the entire initial group should be scheduled when the subgroups have completed their work. This will ensure that everyone is in agreement as to the district's "plan of attack." Once the plan is established, the district policy must be communicated. This communication takes place in the policy meetings.

POLICY MEETING(S)

It is in the policy meetings that the district policy is communicated to the district/school staff. Those presenting this policy would be determined in the follow-up meetings and could include school administrators, the district or school "go-to" person, and possibly an outside expert. Those to whom the policy is communicated would consist of district/school staff, including teachers and other faculty members, administration not included in the presentations, office workers, and any others employed by the school district; interested volunteers, for example the library media center volunteers; and, possibly, students (for example, those high school students who work on the school newspaper and school annual).

At these meetings, it would also be important to cover where this policy would be posted, such as in prominent places in the library media center, computer labs, the teachers' lounge, the school administration office, and in all areas where copy machines, video/audio equipment, etc., are stored and/or used.

AUDITING MEETINGS

While the meetings to establish audit procedures are covered above under "The Follow-up Meeting(s)," there is also an initial audit meeting that is part of the audit process (see Chapter 6).[4]

PROCESS FLOWCHART

Figure 3.2 is the process flowchart, with those boxes highlighted that pertain to this chapter: "Analyze organizational impact of district copyright policy implementation" and "Determine copyright and audit training needs."

It is important to note here that it is absolutely essential for the school administration to support the district copyright compliance policy. It is also essential that the administration support the staff member(s) assigned to administer the policy as well as the school's copyright "go-to" person. If such support does not come from the top down, policy implementation will fail at both the district and the school levels, and the "go-to" person will be in an untenable position.

Let's go back now to the example of our superintendent, whom we talked about earlier in this chapter, the person who wants to make her school district as copyright compliant as it possibly can be. We have seen that she needs to find and/or train external and internal experts and schedule a variety of meetings. Let's elaborate on what she might do, given the copyright compliance process. First of all, we will imagine that she is the top administrative person in her district. In that case, she may have no need to ask permission of other administrators. However, she may need the support of the school board. Once she has received that backing, she begins by considering an external expert. She contacts a university professor who teaches, researches, and writes in the area of school copyright law and asks the professor if he would be willing to come in as an external expert. He agrees. The professor prepares for and manages the initial meeting. At that meeting, together with the district superintendent and other early stakeholders from

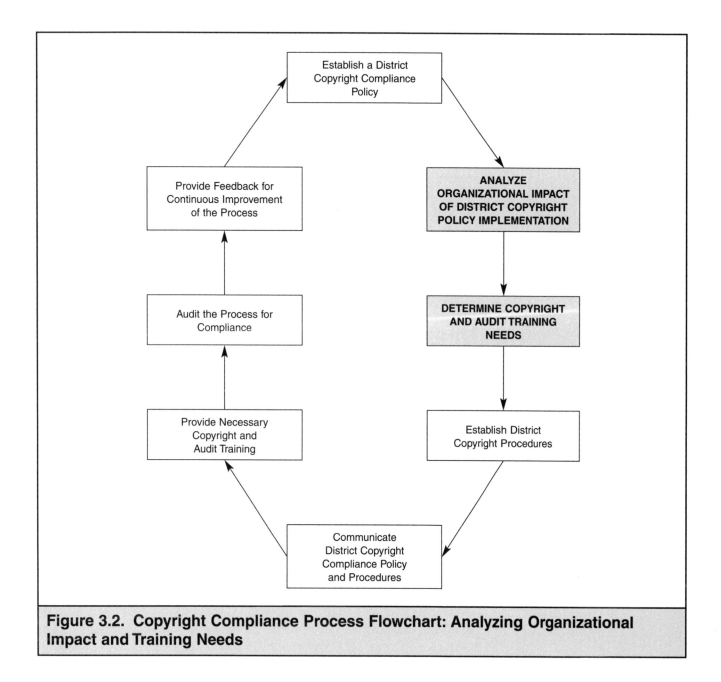

Figure 3.2. Copyright Compliance Process Flowchart: Analyzing Organizational Impact and Training Needs

the district that the superintendent has identified (administrators, school librarians, technology coordinators), discussion first centers on the organizational impact, what needs to be done, who needs to be trained and how, and other issues concerning developing a copyright-compliant school district. The second half of the initial meeting is spent with the professor talking about copyright compliance in general and addressing early copyright questions and concerns. Later meetings with the external expert and the stakeholders address procedural, training, and auditing needs as well as identify who the internal experts and the "go-to" person will be. At this point the policy meetings begin. In these meetings, the district copyright policy (for the purposes of this example, we are assuming that this particular district already has a working copyright policy in place) is communicated to all district administrators, teachers, librarians, and other school faculty and staff. By following the copyright compliance process to this point, our superintendent has gone a long way to ensure that her district does not encounter the same legal problems as the neighboring district that lost its copyright suit.

CONCLUSION

In establishing a copyright compliant process in a school district or school, both external and internal experts may be used. Additionally, there are a number of meetings that are vital to the process, among them the initial and follow-up (procedures, training, and audit-establishing) meetings. The experts will utilize these meetings to facilitate the eight steps of the copyright compliance process. Next we look to Chapter 4 and establishing the copyright procedures.

NOTES

1. Intellectual property "refers to creations of the mind: inventions, literary and artistic works, and symbols, names, images, and designs used in commerce. Intellectual property is divided into two categories: Industrial property, which includes inventions (patents), trademarks, industrial designs, and geographic indications of course; and Copyright, which includes literary and artistic works such as novels, poems and plays, films, musical works, artistic works such as drawings, paintings, photographs and sculptures, and architectural designs. Rights related to copyright include those of performing artists in their performances, producers of phonograms in their recordings, and those of broadcasters in their radio and television programs" (World Intellectual Property Organization, n.d.: 1).
2. Governmental and commercial copyright organizations include those who provide services to both users and owners of copyrighted works. Among these are the U.S. Copyright Office, the Copyright Clearance Center, and Broadcast Music Incorporated (music only).

3. "[A] 'service provider' is defined as a provider of online services or network access, or the operator of facilities therefore, including an entity offering the transmission, routing, or providing of connections for digital online communications, between or among points specified by a user, of material of the user's choosing, without modification to the content of the material as sent or received" (U.S. Copyright Office, 2008: 1).

4. Audit feedback informational support for this chapter comes from personal interviews with Thomas W. Butler, Manufacturing, Plant Engineering, and Maintenance Management Consultant. Butler has been trained to conduct International Organization for Standardization (ISO) audits for commercial and manufacturing environments and has also participated in internal quality audits for several manufacturing companies, including Oscar Mayer Foods Corporation, Kraft Foods Incorporated, and OSI Food Company.

REFERENCES

U.S. Copyright Office. 2008. "Online Service Providers." Available: www.copyright.gov/onlinesp/ (accessed October 15, 2008).

World Intellectual Property Organization. n.d. "What is Intellectual Property?" Available: www.wipo.int/about-ip/en/ (accessed July 15, 2008).

4 COPYRIGHT PROCEDURES

INTRODUCTION

Let's go back to our copyright compliance example from Chapter 2, the school district with no copyright policy, one that has not been updated in many years, or one that appears incomplete. Well, once that policy is written, revised, and/or updated, then it is necessary to address the procedures that will help make the school district copyright policy work. A district may already have some copyright procedures in place. If this is not the case, then procedures should be developed and/or modified in order to meet the new policy. These procedures also need to be presented to the district share-holders (administrators, school librarians, technology coordinators, teachers, and others). Additionally, a school within the district may establish its own procedures that it follows in order to abide by the district policy. Thus, the focus of this chapter is on school/school district copyright procedures. In this chapter, the procedures needed to enforce the policy as well as how to write and communicate these procedural items are defined, detailed, and discussed.

Figure 4.1 is the copyright compliance process flowchart. The procedural step "Establish district copyright procedures" is highlighted. Please note that the fifth step, "Communicate district copyright compliance policy and procedures," is also highlighted because it is addressed later in this chapter as it connects to copyright procedures.

SCHOOL DISTRICT COPYRIGHT PROCEDURES: DEFINITION AND AUDIENCE

According to the *Merriam-Webster Online Dictionary* (2008), a procedure is "a particular way of accomplishing something or of acting," "a series of steps followed in a regular definite order," or "a traditional or established way of doing things." For our specific needs, copyright procedures are instituted by a particular school district in order to ensure that the district copyright policy is followed correctly.

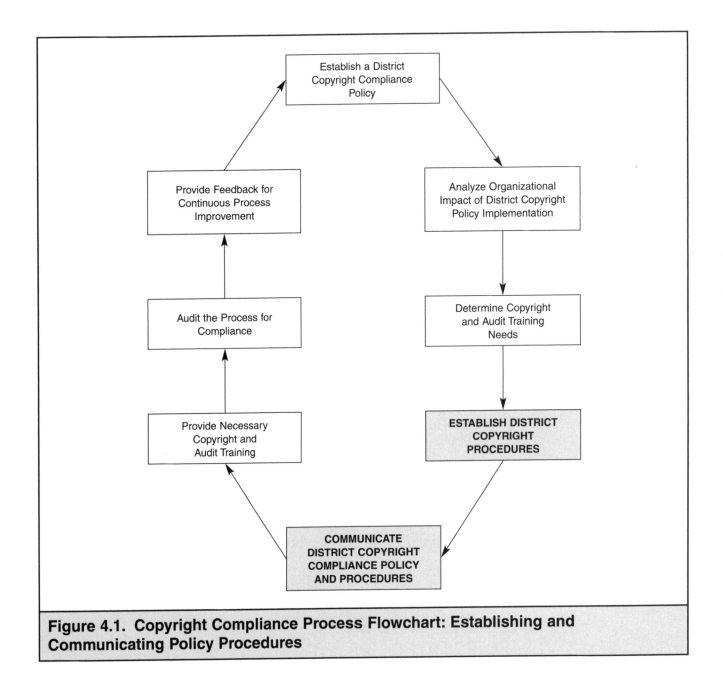

Figure 4.1. Copyright Compliance Process Flowchart: Establishing and Communicating Policy Procedures

The audience for school district copyright procedures is the same audience as that for the copyright policy: the stakeholders—librarians, technology specialists/coordinators, teachers, administrators, copy center personnel, and other school district employees. Students in the district might also make up part of the procedures' audience; however, this depends on the students' use of works, since K–12 students may copy more than librarians, teachers, and other school district employees when such copying is needed to achieve a particular instructional objective (Butler, 2004; U.S. Copyright Law, 1976).

CONTENT AND LOCATION OF DISTRICT-WIDE COPYRIGHT PROCEDURES

What belongs in copyright procedures can vary from district to district, as can what is in the copyright policy itself. In general, copyright procedures cover how to put the district copyright policies into effect; for example, discussing how to get permission from a copyright owner or how to report a copyright violation.

There is no one area to look for those procedures that implement school district copyright policies. Sometimes procedures are written into the policy; that is, they are part of the copyright policy itself. In this case, procedures may be an identified category within the policy ("Copyright Policy & Procedures for Hopkins School District 270," 1995) or may be scattered throughout the policy, but not identified as procedural ("A Quick Reference Employee Copyright Handbook," 2003). It is also possible that copyright procedures are another document found with or in addition to the policy ("Copyright Compliance—Annual Audit," n.d.), or are inferred/assumed by the school stakeholders but never written down. It is best to ensure that all stakeholders can easily find copyright compliance procedures. Thus, either a separate but attached document to the copyright policy or a defined part of the policy is recommended for copyright procedures. These can be in print or on the Internet. This is discussed later in the chapter.

Examples demonstrating the various types of school district procedures commonly found are presented next.

PROCEDURES AS PART OF THE COPYRIGHT POLICY

The following examples are found within current school district copyright policies.

Identified Procedural Category Within the Copyright Policy

See sidebar.

Procedures Scattered Throughout the Policy but Not Identified as Procedural

The label in Figure 4.2 is found in a copyright policy. It is an example of a notice that can be placed near equipment that copies works or it can be posted near a copying center. It appears in the copyright policy with no

---

Copyright—Computer Software

The following procedures represent a sincere effort to comply with copyright laws:

1. District 270 equipment may not be used for making illegal copies of software.

2. A copyright reminder label will be attached to each computer.

3. The use of illegally copied software in schools or offices is prohibited.

4. Software licensing agreements of copyright holders must be observed.

Source: "Copyright Policy & Procedures for Hopkins School District 270" (1995: 5).

Copyright

©

- The copyright law of the United States (Title 17 U.S. Code) governs the making of photocopies or other reproductions of copyrighted material.
- This institution reserves the right to refuse to accept a copying order if, in its judgment, fulfillment of the order would involve violation of copyright law.

Figure 4.2. Copyright Label for Posting Near Equipment That Copies or in a Copying Center

---

instructions as to its use. Thus it is assumed, by the policy authors, that those stakeholders who read the label will know how to use it.[1]

COPYRIGHT PROCEDURES AS A DOCUMENT IN ADDITION TO THE POLICY

An example of a copyright procedure that could be a stand-alone document is that of a series of questions to be used when considering copying a work. The school librarian might post these in flowchart form near equipment (photocopy machines, computers, video recorders, etc.) that is used to copy works (see Figure 4.3). The idea behind this posting would be to encourage equipment users to think before arbitrarily copying.

INFERRED/ASSUMED COPYRIGHT PROCEDURES

Inferred/assumed procedures are not written down; instead, the author(s) of the copyright policy assume(s) that those who read the policy will act in such a way as to ensure copyright compliance because of the policy they have read.

QUESTIONS TO CONSIDER WHEN DEVELOPING COPYRIGHT COMPLIANCE PROCEDURES

In addition to the procedures discussed previously (those sometimes found or inferred in existing copyright procedure or policy documents), your

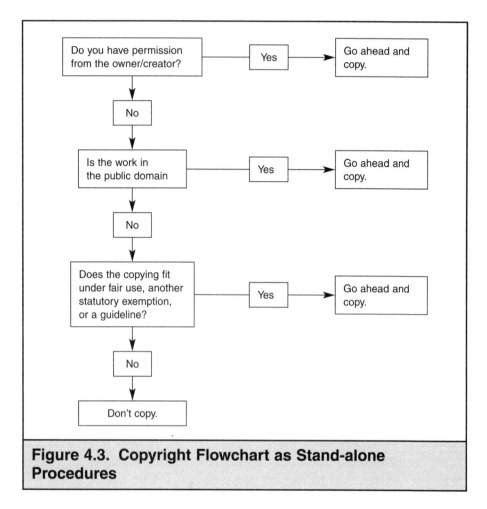

Figure 4.3. Copyright Flowchart as Stand-alone Procedures

copyright procedures will specifically address the goal of this book: school district and school copyright compliance. As a result, the following questions demonstrate the types of things that should also be found in your procedural document:

- Who are your experts?
- How will they be chosen?
- Who will be trained in copyright compliance?
- How will these individuals be trained?
- What will they be trained in?
- Who will communicate the district copyright policy?
- Who will be the district "go-to" person?
- Who will be the school "go-to" person?
- Who and where will copyright violations be reported?
- How will copyright violations be reported?

- How often will copyright compliance in the district/school be audited?
- Who will do the auditing?
- How often will feedback be provided?
- Who will provide the feedback and to whom will it be provided?
- How will the feedback be provided?
- How often should the district copyright policy be reviewed?
- Who should review the district copyright policy?
- Who will model copyright compliance to district employees?
- Who will model copyright compliance to school district students?

Please note that these questions and answers are covered throughout this book, many specifically in Chapter 3.

Sample procedures for each of these questions are provided next: first the question is listed; after it is an example of what might go in your copyright compliance policy given that particular query.

1. **Who are your experts?**
   Copyright compliance experts can be internal—school librarians, technology specialists, or administrators, or external—intellectual property lawyers or university professors who teach and/or research in copyright law. All such individuals need to be articulate and current in copyright law and its issues.

2. **How will experts be chosen?**
   The superintendent and assistant superintendent will select internal and external copyright compliance experts.

3. **Who will be trained in copyright compliance?**
   All district and individual school staff (administrators, teachers, school library media specialists, technology specialists, secretaries and other administrative support staff, teachers' aides, etc.) will be trained in copyright compliance.

4. **How will individuals be trained in copyright compliance?**
   Current district and individual school staff will be trained in copyright compliance during the first year of its inception. After that, annual reviews will be held during one of the fall in-service days. All new district and individual school staff will be trained in copyright

compliance during their first year of employment, with yearly reviews to follow.

5. **What exactly will individuals be trained in?**
   All district and individual school staff will be trained in the use and understanding of the district copyright policy and in the importance of the policy to their particular school environment.

6. **Who will communicate the district copyright policy?**
   The district copyright policy and additional copyright material will be communicated to all district and individual school staff by the internal and external experts.

7. **Who will be the district "go-to" person?**
   The district copyright compliance "go-to" person will be the assistant superintendent.

8. **Who will be the school "go-to" person?**
   The school copyright compliance "go-to" person will be the building librarian. If this person is unable to function in this capacity, then the building technology specialist will take over this position.

9. **Who will copyright violations be reported to?**
   School copyright violations will be reported to the school "go-to" person or, in the case of online infringements, to the online service provider agent. District level copyright violations will be reported to the district "go-to" person and/or the online service provider agent.

10. **How will copyright violations be reported?**
    Both the district and school "go-to" people/online service provider agents will receive notice of copyright infringements occurring in their building(s) via a report form available in all administration offices. Infringements can also be reported via e-mail or phone.

11. **How often will copyright compliance in the district/school be audited?**
    The district and each individual school will be audited for copyright compliance annually.

12. **Who will do the auditing?**
    Auditing will be done by external experts selected by the district administration and school board.

13. **How often will feedback be provided?**
    Feedback from the audit will be provided to all stakeholders (district and school staff) annually, after the audit has taken place.

14. Who will provide the feedback and to whom will it be provided?

Annual feedback will be provided to the stakeholders by the external expert(s) who conducted the audit.

15. How will feedback be provided?

Feedback will be provided to all stakeholders verbally in an in-service, after the audit has taken place, and also in a written report that will be given to each individual. This feedback will also be situated on the district Web site.

16. How often should the district copyright policy be reviewed?

The district copyright policy will be reviewed annually or whenever there is a major change in the federal copyright law.

17. Who should review the district copyright policy?

Internal and external experts will review the district copyright policy. Both groups are required to keep abreast of copyright law as part of their professional responsibilities.

18. Who will model copyright compliance to district employees?

Internal and external experts will model copyright compliance to all district and individual school employees. In addition, district and school employees will model copyright compliance at all times with one another.

19. Who will model copyright compliance to school district students?

Copyright compliance will be modeled to school district students by all district and individual school staff, in particular (1) school administrators, such as principals; (2) school librarians; (3) technology specialists; and (4) teachers.

The following illustration of copyright compliance procedures for the central administration office, schools, and district staff hails from a private (religious) education office in Australia. Nonetheless, its points fit well into what we are talking about in this chapter and can be applied to both the public and private school environments in the United States:

The following checklists are designed to . . . minimize the risk of infringement . . . [The school administration]

• Provides support material and in-service to help schools and staff comply with their copyright obligations

- Places relevant warning and limits notices on all school copying equipment—photocopiers, scanners, computers, VCRs and other audio-visual equipment

("Copyright Compliance—Annual Audit," n.d., 1)

HOW TO WRITE COPYRIGHT PROCEDURES

WORKING WITH EXISTING COPYRIGHT PROCEDURES

Existing copyright procedures may or may not exist in your district. If available, they may be old and unusable. Once they are accessed, the copyright policy committee needs to read the procedures over carefully to determine if those existing contain what is necessary to support the copyright policy. Depending on the decision, the committee can then decide to rewrite, add to, or keep the copyright procedures.

WRITING NEW COPYRIGHT PROCEDURES

Just as with copyright policy, there is no one means to writing or creating copyright procedures. First of all, a group or individual who appears to be able to start and complete such a project is needed; for instance, the same committee or person as the one who wrote the copyright policy might also write up the procedures. The writer(s) might also study what other schools have already done; find and refer to information from a wide variety of educational and copyright sources, such as professional organizational information, copyright material on the Web and in books, etc.; and use professionals, such as copyright lawyers or other copyright experts. Last, just like the copyright policy, copyright procedures should also be written in a concise and understandable manner.

Who Writes the Procedures?

Those who write and/or revise copyright procedures can vary from district to district. Often they are the same people who wrote the copyright policy. Whatever the case may be, it is important that those who work on the procedures are knowledgeable in copyright law and its application within K–12 educational settings. People within the district who might be on a procedures' committee include school administrators, librarians, technology specialists, and teachers, and also a member of the school board or a school attorney. Like the copyright policy committee discussed in Chapter 2, while the procedures' committee can be composed of representative individuals, it should not be so large as to be unwieldy. It is important to go with what works best in your district, whether this is a small group or even an individual rather than a committee. In some cases, a subgroup, perhaps of school librarians who have taken a copyright class, might write up working procedures. These are then presented to the main committee for review, discussion, and revisions. Eventually the final procedures are submitted to the school board (and, depending on your district, the school administration) for approval.

PROCEDURAL COMMUNICATION AND TRAINING

School district copyright compliance procedures should be communicated to *all* employees verbally, as a part of the formal meetings at the start of each school year as well as a part of all new employee orientations (see Chapter 3). The procedures should also be accessible online, in an easily reached location, on the school Web page, a district file server, or a school intranet (accessible only to district employees). Where it is available depends on the wishes of the school district stakeholders and the recommendations of the external and internal experts.

All district employees should receive training on copyright compliance procedures at the same time as the copyright policy training, that is, annually or whenever the policy and procedures are changed. Procedural training can be done by the same individuals who do the policy training: an internal expert (someone within the district who has received adequate copyright law training and who is familiar with the district copyright policy) or by an external expert who is a copyright authority and has reviewed and/or approved the district policy.

CONCLUSION

In this chapter, we looked at copyright compliance procedures, what they are, how they are created, who their audience is, and how they are communicated. These procedures are important in that they tell us *how* we will follow copyright policy. In the next chapter, we focus on training as it pertains to copyright policy and procedures and the audit process.

NOTES

1. Interestingly, both of the examples (identified procedures and unidentified procedures) are found in the same school district copyright policy—just on different pages!

REFERENCES

Butler, Rebecca P. 2004. *Copyright for Teachers and Librarians*. New York: Neal-Schuman.

"Copyright Compliance—Annual Audit." n.d. Diocese of Townsville, Australia: Catholic Education. Available: www.tsv.catholic.edu.au/documents/Copyright%20Compliance.pdf (accessed August 16, 2008).

"Copyright Policy & Procedures for Hopkins School District 270." 1995. Hopkins, MN: Board of Education.

Merriam-Webster Online Dictionary. 2008. s.v. "Procedures." Available: www.merriam-webster.com/dictionary/procedures (accessed August 12, 2008).

"A Quick Reference Employee Copyright Handbook." 2003. Rosemount, MN: Independent School District 196.

U.S. Copyright Law. 1976. Public Law 94-553.

5 TRAINING

INTRODUCTION

The process continues to evolve—external and/or internal experts have met with stakeholders, initial meetings and policy meetings have been held. It is now time to determine the identity of the trainer(s) as well as address training: who, what, when, where, and how to train. Such steps need to be done so that stakeholders have a working understanding of basic copyright compliance and the district copyright policy. In addition, those chosen to be auditors must comprehend how to perform an audit (see Figure 5.1).

SELECTING YOUR TRAINER

Who should train the school/district employees? The flowchart in Figure 5.2 illustrates the steps necessary in deciding whether the copyright compliance trainer will be external or internal. Following the flowchart is information covering the trainer decision points.

Next we look to who, what, when, where, and how to train.

WHO TO TRAIN

Those to be trained are the stakeholders, district and school employees, administration, school librarians, technology specialists, teachers, paraprofessionals, copy center employees, office staff, and eventually the students. Some of these individuals will be trained as the internal experts, the "go-to" people and/or those who collect infringement reports for the district and individual schools (such as the online service provider agent), and still others may be trained as auditors. Additionally, the majority of the stakeholders (district employees) will be trained in general copyright compliance, the district policy, and procedures. Training needs to be both *initial* and *ongoing* for all groups. Initial training will cover any introductory material as well as the basic information needed for K–12 copyright compliance and

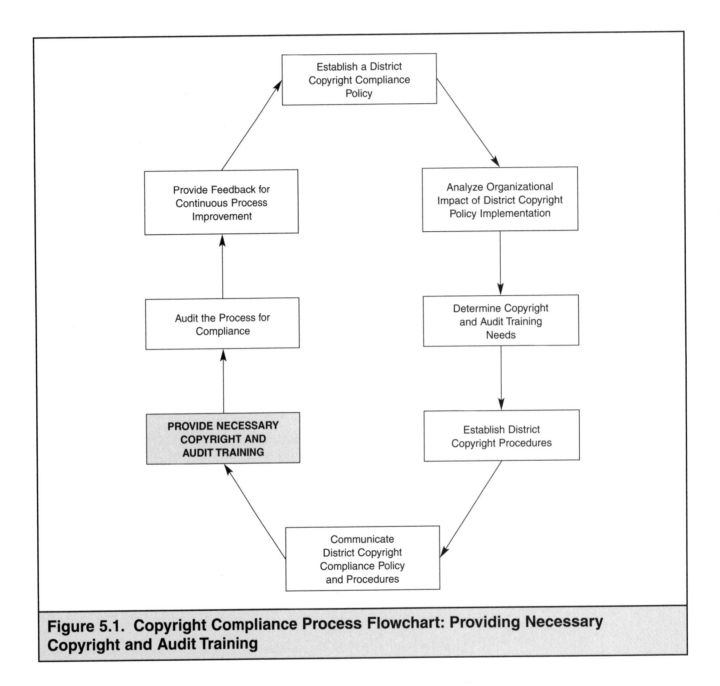

Figure 5.1. Copyright Compliance Process Flowchart: Providing Necessary Copyright and Audit Training

knowledge of the district copyright policy. Ongoing training will maintain currency in both of these areas.

INTERNAL EXPERTS

The internal experts may be those with some background and/or interest in school and copyright law. Thus, a strong district internal expert might be a

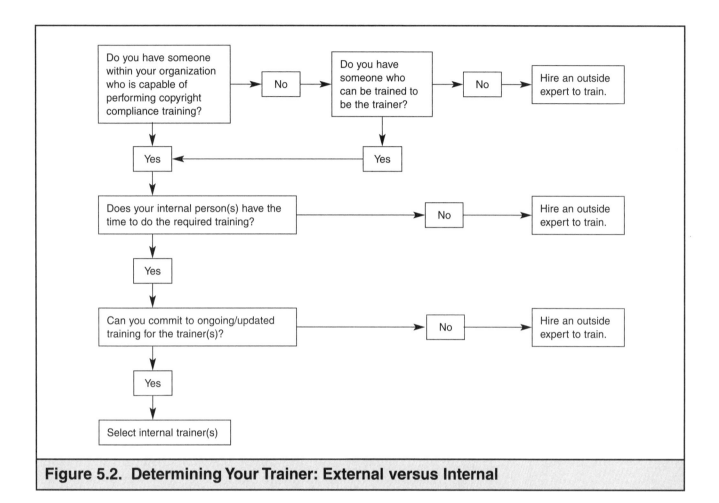

Figure 5.2. Determining Your Trainer: External versus Internal

The flowchart for selecting your copyright compliance trainer(s) has several decision points. The following briefly describes each decision point and its importance:

Decision 1: Do you have someone in your organization who is capable of performing copyright compliance training? A qualified internal person would be one who has a working knowledge of copyright law as it applies to the schools in your district. This person should also be very knowledgeable of your district copyright compliance policy since the required training encompasses both copyright law and your district policy. In addition, this individual should be someone who enjoys training, because this will make them more effective.

Decision 2: Do you have someone who can be trained to be the trainer? If you don't already have someone qualified, there may be someone in your organization who can be trained to take on this role. They should be capable of obtaining sufficient knowledge of both copyright law and your district policy in order to teach others. As mentioned with Decision 1, this person should also be someone who enjoys training.

Decision 3: Does your internal person(s) have the time to do the required training? In all likelihood, the person(s) you have in mind to be the trainer already has a full schedule. It is important to realize that this position will require time above and beyond the person's normal job duties. Depending on the size of your school and district, this time commitment could be substantial. This person(s) will be conducting initial and

(Cont'd.)

ongoing classes, which will require both preparation and actual classroom time. In addition, the would-be trainer(s) will need to remain current in both the law and your district policy.

Decision 4: Can you commit to ongoing/updated training for the trainer(s)? As mentioned, this individual(s) will be required to stay current in both copyright law and your district policy. This may require them to attend refresher classes, which will most likely mean time away from their normal job as well as additional costs to the district. This requires a commitment on the part of the district to make both the time and money available for the internal trainer(s).

If the answer to any of the questions above is "no," then turn to an external trainer.

school administrator, a school library media specialist, or a technology specialist. This is because these individuals are often required to take at least one course in school law or ethics as part of their college/university classes (Northern Illinois University, 2007; University of Wisconsin–Madison, 2008). It is important to remember here that the internal experts and/or external experts are those who train the "go-to" people, online service provider agents, auditors, and general district employee population.

"GO-TO" PEOPLE AND ONLINE SERVICE PROVIDER AGENTS

For most school districts, as well as individual schools, it is probably least confusing if the person who can help others with copyright questions and information and the person who collects reports of copyright infringements are the same person—the "go-to" person. Remember that for online copyright infringements, all reports need to go to the designated online service provider agent. "Go-to" people and/or online service provider agents can be separate individuals, or the same, whichever the school district finds more amenable. Once again, while such individuals could be any district employees, the strongest "go-to" people and/or online service provider agents are those with a background and interest in school law, especially copyright law. Thus, those who normally have training and work in these areas come to the forefront: school librarians, technology specialists, and school administrators. However, there may be teachers in individual schools who are also strong or who are willing to work and learn in the area of copyright compliance. It would be best to first ask for those who express interest. Copyright compliance can be a complicated process; thus, it is important to identify someone with the interest and the willingness to become an expert.

AUDITORS

Auditing training involves identifying how, when, where, who, and what to audit. Since the audit is the step in the copyright compliance process that ensures that the district is adhering to its compliance policy, the importance of this training must not be underestimated. (This information is covered in Chapter 6.)

DISTRICT EMPLOYEES IN GENERAL

It is important that those district and individual school administrators, faculty, and staff who are not internal experts, "go-to" people, or auditors are trained and kept updated in the basics of copyright compliancy. Such individuals are the main group who work with and use materials as well as model and inform their students concerning the basics of borrowing and copying in a legal and ethical manner. It is important that *all* in the schools and school district understand copyright compliancy.

WHAT TO TRAIN

What information internal experts, "go-to" people, auditors, and district employees in general need to know about copyright compliancy depends on their particular group's responsibilities. All groups need to know the following:

- Copyright law as it relates to K–12 education and the areas of emphasis of each employee (for example, a school librarian would specifically want to understand copyright law as it pertains to copying in the library)
- The school district copyright compliance process
- The school district copyright policy and procedures
- Professional standards that cover copyright compliance
- Where to go for additional copyright information
- How to work with those who would infringe
- How to report infringements

Samples of each of these follow.

SAMPLE K–12 COPYRIGHT LAW

The following is an excerpt from copyright law as it informs the reproduction of library materials.

(a) Except as otherwise provided in this title and notwithstanding the provisions of section 106, it is not an infringement of copyright for a library or archives, or any of its employees acting within the scope of their employment, to reproduce no more than one copy or phonorecord of a work, except as provided in subsections (b) and (c), or to distribute such copy or phonorecord, under the conditions specified by this section, if—

(1) the reproduction or distribution is made without any purpose of direct or indirect commercial advantage;

(2) the collections of the library or archives are (i) open to the public, or (ii) available not only to researchers affiliated with the library or archives or with the institution of which it is a part, but also to other persons doing research in a specialized field; and

(3) the reproduction or distribution of the work includes a notice of copyright that appears on the copy or phonorecord that is reproduced under the provisions of this section, or includes a legend stating that the work may be protected by copyright if no such notice can be found on the copy or phonorecord that is reproduced under the provisions of this section . . .

Source: "Copyright Law of the United States: Section 108" (2007).

SAMPLE SCHOOL DISTRICT COPYRIGHT COMPLIANCE PROCESS

See Chapter 3 of this book.

SAMPLE SCHOOL DISTRICT COPYRIGHT POLICY AND PROCEDURES

The following example pertains to copyright and placing materials on the Web.

No use of corporate logos or derivative works is allowed unless written permission has been granted. . . . Graphics/sounds from contemporary films/TV shows may not be used without copyright permission. . . . Claiming ignorance is not acceptable; be sure about your right to use material and document it. . . . Original material is encouraged as being the most authentic and of the most interest to the districts/schools' stakeholders. . . . Web pages may NOT contain content unless the author can show ownership or permission.

Source: "Network Facilities and Internet Access" (2001: 3).

For more policy examples, see Tool V in the "Compliance Toolkit."

SAMPLE PROFESSIONAL STANDARDS ADDRESSING COPYRIGHT COMPLIANCE

Most professional educational organizations have standards, and some of these address copyright and other intellectual property issues. The following is an excerpt from the American Association of School Librarians' *Standards for the 21st-Century Learner*:

---

3. Share knowledge and participate ethically and productively as members of our democratic society.

  3.1 Skills

    3.1.6 Use information and technology ethically and responsibly

  3.3 Responsibilities

    3.3.6 Use information and knowledge in the service of democratic values

Source: Standards for the 21st-Century Learner (2007: 6).

SAMPLE ADDITIONAL COPYRIGHT INFORMATION

Copyright information is massive and varied. It can be anything dealing with copyright and can be found in any number of places (see also Tools V, VI, and VII in the "Compliance Toolkit"). For our purposes in this book, three examples are used: a piece of a "reader's agreement" from a book, part of a database copyright statement, and a statement from a newsletter article.

Reader's Agreement

> You agree not to reproduce, replicate, or reprint any of the material in this book without our consent. (Rosenthall, 2005, v)

Database Copyright Statement

> Temporary storage of output from an online search is permitted for purposes of subsequent editing. Practices such as combining and duplicating results from multidatabase searches, and storing copies of results for personal use of for one-time delivery to a single client, solely for the client's own internal use, is recognized as fair and valid use of material. ("Database Information, Disclaimer, and Copyright Statements," n.d.: 2)

Periodical Article

Periodical articles vary in content and information. Articles speaking to copyright and K–12 education are, like other works about copyright, plentiful.

If we are unable to find the owner of a work, how do we contact them for permission to use or copy their work(s)? Well, we can go to the publisher of the work for contact information. We also can go to an organization, such as an agency or royalty house, company, or clearinghouse that specializes in helping users obtain copyright clearance. Such a group, usually for a fee, will work with us to obtain the proper clearance or license that we need to use a particular medium. Thus depending on the type of media that we need permission to use or copy, where we go to find permission information may vary.

Source: Butler, "Obtaining Permission to Copy or Perform a Work" (2007: 62).

SAMPLE WORKING WITH THOSE WHO WOULD INFRINGE

> Please report all infringements that you observe to [the school "go-to" person].

SAMPLE HOW TO REPORT INFRINGEMENTS

> Please complete the Infringement Report. This report is available in the school district office, all school administration offices, and all school libraries. You do not need to sign the form. Reports may be made anonymously.

In addition to the training that all district employees require, "go-to" people and auditors must receive additional specific training. "Go-to" people (and online service provider agents) need additional instruction in how to deal with copyright questions and concerns brought to them by the general school and district employee population as well as in how to record and report copyright infringements that are reported to and/or observed by them. For example, a "go-to" person might be counseled by his or her trainer to react to all questions, concerns, and perceived copyright violations in a calming manner in order to ensure that the person asking the question or accused of copyright infringement does not feel threatened.

Auditors require specialized training in the performance of an audit (see Chapter 6), and internal experts who may also act as "go-to" people/online service provider agents, auditors, and those who "train the trainers" need instruction in *all* areas under discussion in this book, including knowledge of how to train others in copyright law as it pertains to elementary and secondary education. (Internal experts may already have information, such as copyright activities, instructional materials, etc., gained through the external experts, workshops, college classes, and more.)

WHEN TO TRAIN

Chapter 3 addresses when to train in detail. However, all stakeholders need to obtain initial training to inform and introduce them to the copyright compliancy process and ongoing instruction to keep them current in copyright law and the corresponding K–12 issues. As pointed out in Chapter 3, initial training for new employees should occur as part of their new employee orientation.

WHERE TO TRAIN

The training venue depends on the particular school district and participating schools. Conversely, generally internal experts, "go to" people, and auditors are trained on the district level, while the internal and/or external experts train school employees in their individual schools.

HOW TO TRAIN

Training in copyright compliancy can be accomplished in a number of ways. Those who are first trained need to be the internal experts. These individuals may be trained by the external experts or through workshops, college classes, and more. The internal (and perhaps external experts) can then begin training other district and school stakeholders. Auditors, also, are more likely to be trained by external personnel, workshops, etc. In general, auditor training would be enhanced by allowing the auditor-in-training to accompany an experienced auditor on an actual compliance audit.

TRAINING MATERIALS

The materials used to train the various individuals and groups that make up the school district stakeholders can be many and varied. Once again, outside personnel may provide information. In addition, training materials can be found via the following:

- World Wide Web
- Books
- Articles
- Copyright classes and workshops
- Resources such as the copyright law: www.copyright.gov/title17/

See Tools V, VI, and VII in the "Compliance Toolkit" for places to obtain copyright compliance training materials. See Tool I for examples of copyright compliance training materials.

CONCLUSION

The chapter speaks to training the various school and district stakeholders as to what is needed concerning their positions on the copyright compliance team. Everyone in the school district, and the schools that make up the district, needs such training; what, when, where, and how much depends on their responsibilities within the copyright compliance process. It naturally follows that the more effective the training, the more likely the district will become and remain copyright compliant.

REFERENCES

Butler, Rebecca P. 2007. "Obtaining Permission to Copy or Perform a Work, Part III, Revised 2006." *Knowledge Quest* 35, no. 5: 62–64.

"Copyright Law of the United States: Section 108. Limitations on Exclusive Rights: Reproduction by Libraries and Archives." 2007. Washington, DC: U.S. Copyright Office. Available: www.copyright .gov/title17/ (accessed August 21, 2008).

"Database Information, Disclaimer, and Copyright Statements." n.d. Albuquerque, NM: National Information Center for Educational Media. Available: http://accessinn.com/plweb/NICEM/dbdef.html (accessed August 28, 2008).

"Network Facilities and Internet Access." 2001. Arlington Heights, IL: Township High School District 214.

Northern Illinois University. 2007. *Northern Illinois University Graduate Catalog 2007–2008*. Dekalb, IL: Northern Illinois University.

Rosenthall, Amy Krouse. 2005. *Encyclopedia of an Ordinary Life*. Volume 1. New York: Crown Publishers.

Standards for the 21st-Century Learner. 2007. Chicago, IL: American Association of School Librarians. Available: www.ala.org/ala/aasl/ aaslproftools/learningstandards/standards.cfm (accessed August 28, 2008).

University of Wisconsin–Madison. 2008. *University of Wisconsin–Madison Graduate School Catalog*. Madison, WI: University of Wisconsin-Madison. Available: www.wisc.edu/grad/ catalog/fields.html (accessed August 28, 2008).

6

AUDITING THE COPYRIGHT COMPLIANCE PROCESS

INTRODUCTION

Let's assume that you are the "go-to" person in a school participating in a district-wide copyright compliance initiative. The audit is imminent, and your school's teachers are asking you what is going to happen with this part of the process. What can you tell them?

Once the copyright compliance process, procedures, and training are completed and the process is in place, the next step is to audit what is happening. Much as lesson plans have a piece that looks to see how well the students have responded to the lesson (an assessment), or the "Big6™"[1] has "evaluation" as its sixth and last step, so, too, does the copyright compliance process have an audit. The audit is used to determine if and how well the process is being followed. This step (audit) is related to providing feedback (see Chapter 7) given that an audit must be developed and conducted in order to obtain the feedback desired. Figure 6.1 illustrates Step 5: Audit the process for copyright compliance (highlighted in flowchart).

This chapter, therefore, (1) defines the audit process, (2) explains the audit meetings, (3) discusses auditing procedures, (4) gives examples of criteria needed in auditing materials as well as sample audit sheets, (5) identifies auditors, and (6) covers conducting an audit.

DEFINING THE AUDIT PROCESS

Audit as used in this book, means "a systematic check or assessment, especially of the efficiency or effectiveness of an organization or department, typically carried out by an independent assessor" (*Encarta World English Dictionary*, 1999). Thus, the audit is to make sure that the copyright policy is in place and copyright compliance is being followed in the district or school under audit. In this case, the district (and each school within it) is audited separately so as to determine compliancy under both copyright law and the district's established copyright policy.

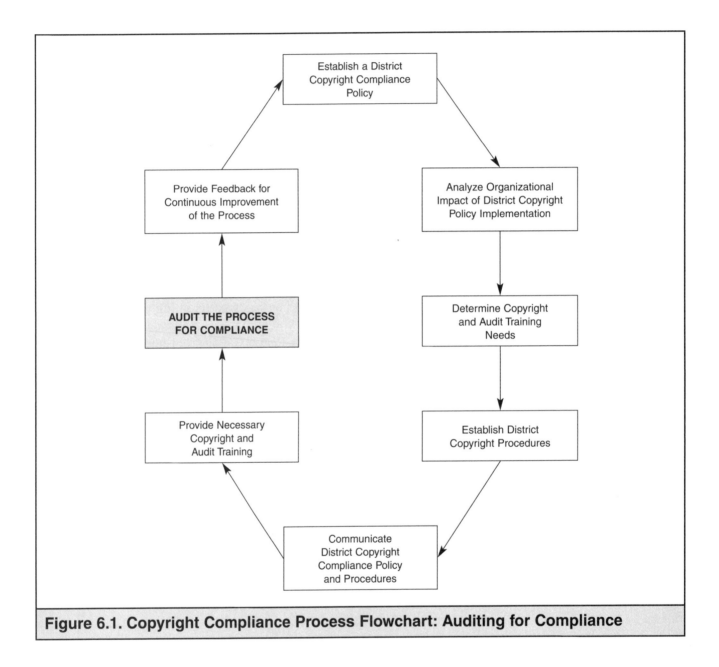

Figure 6.1. Copyright Compliance Process Flowchart: Auditing for Compliance

AUDIT MEETINGS

There are two meetings in conjunction with the audit part of the copyright compliance process: the initial audit meeting and the closing audit meeting. The initial audit meeting occurs as the first step of an audit. In this case, the auditor meets with the district or school administration "go-to" person, the online service provider agent, as well as any other personnel who will make available information for the audit (i.e., those being audited). Any of these individuals might include the school librarians, curriculum coordinators, technology specialists, teachers, and students. This meeting is for the purpose of describing what will happen during the audit, establishing a schedule for meeting with those who will be audited, and to schedule a closing meeting to review the results of the audit. The closing audit meeting is conducted by the auditor and can be attended by all those audited.

QUESTIONS TO CONSIDER WHEN DEVELOPING AUDIT PROCEDURES

The primary purpose for conducting the audit is to ensure that the school system is in compliance with the district's copyright policy and, therefore, copyright law. However, audits have the added benefits of providing the basis for continuous improvement of the district policy and showing the district's good intentions to comply with copyright law. In order to perform the audit, particular guidelines and procedures need to be developed and followed. Typical questions that must be answered (remember that you may have something that is particular to your district or school that also needs addressing) are the following:

- Who will perform the audit?
- Who will be audited?
- What will be asked of those audited?
- Where will the audit take place?
- When will the audit occur?

WHO WILL CONDUCT THE AUDIT?

The audit may be conducted by an outside auditor or consultant (see Figure 6.2). This is often preferred because an outside auditor is less likely to be biased in regard to the organization under audit and also because the outside auditor is an expert in what he or she is doing. A second possibility is an internal auditor, someone who is part of the district—for example, the district media person, online service provider agent, or an individual from a school other than the one under audit. If using someone from another school, the risk of a hidden agenda, the urge of the auditor to make sure that his or her school comes out looking better than the one he or she is auditing, is always a possibility. Therefore, external auditors are encouraged. Also, when using an internal auditor, that person, unless already a copyright expert, will need to be trained in both copyright compliance and auditing procedures. This brings up the issue of who will train the auditor. Ideas include sending the internal auditor to specialized conferences, training sessions, etc., on copyright compliance, in order to receive the information that he or she needs. Another auditing idea is for a team approach, where the team is comprised of both outside and internal auditors, thus potentially overcoming internal bias while at the same time being able to understand on a local level those being audited. For example, the team could be composed of a college law professor with an expertise in copyright (the external auditor), the librarian at one of the schools being audited (an internal expert), and so on. While any of these approaches will work, in the case of copyright compliancy, an outside copyright expert/professional auditor or the team approach is recommended.

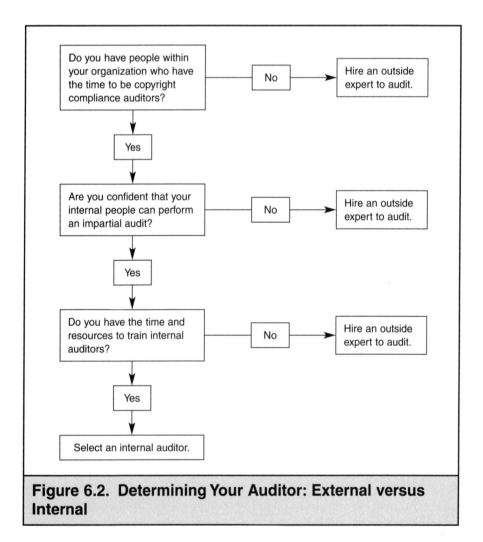

Figure 6.2. Determining Your Auditor: External versus Internal

The flowchart for selecting your copyright compliance auditors has several decision points. The following briefly describes each decision point and its importance:

Decision 1: Do you have people within your organization who have the time to be copyright auditors? In all likelihood, the people you have in mind for auditors already have a full schedule. It is important to realize that this position will require time above and beyond the person's normal job duties. Depending on the size of your school and district, this time commitment could be substantial. The people selected will require initial and ongoing training on the auditing process as well as on your district copyright compliance policy. In addition, since the district office and every school in the district will be audited on a continuous basis, the time commitment for the auditors will continue for as long as they are involved with auditing.

Decision 2: Are you confident that your internal people can perform an impartial audit? In most cases this will not be an issue. It is important to note, however, that for the audit process to be effective and provide the compliance assurance you seek, it is critical that your auditors be completely impartial. You can't make good decisions with poor information.

Decision 3: Do you have the time and resources to train internal auditors? As mentioned, people selected to be auditors will require initial and ongoing training. Someone will have to do this training. Regardless of whether this is done internally or externally, it will require time and funding on an ongoing basis.

If the answer to any of the questions above is "no," hire an external auditor.

WHO WILL BE AUDITED?

Those to be audited are those who are included in the district's copyright policy. On the district level, this would be the district administrators, technology specialists, district media/school library coordinator, and similar individuals. On the school/building level, those audited would include the principal and other building administrators, the building library media specialist(s) and technology coordinator(s), the teachers, and support staff. Although it is imperative that students also be trained in copyright compliancy, their auditing is part of the curriculum and thus not addressed here.

WHAT WILL BE ASKED OF THOSE AUDITED?

Generally speaking, a copyright compliance audit sheet includes statements such as the following, with accompanying sections for responses of "yes" or "no," "true" or "false," or something similar. Additionally, audit sheets should also include a section for actions required (if any) for each audit item:

- A copyright compliance policy has been established.
- The copyright compliance policy is reviewed on a regular basis to ensure currency.
- The copyright compliance policy has been communicated to all appropriate employees.

- Training on the copyright compliance policy is provided to all appropriate employees on a regular basis.
- Training on the copyright compliance policy is provided to all appropriate new employees as part of their initial orientation.
- All copyright compliance policy training is documented.
- A copyright "expert" has been established. Appropriate employees are aware of the identity of this person.
- The copyright "expert" has been trained on and is current in copyright law as it pertains to all areas of focus.
- The copyright compliance audit is conducted on a regular basis. Results of the audit are communicated to appropriate personnel.
- Follow-up action items are completed in a timely manner and completion is documented.

WHERE WILL THE AUDIT TAKE PLACE?

The audit should take place at the district office for district personnel and in the individual schools for building personnel so that the auditor can verify such things as (1) that the policy is posted, (2) proper training has taken place, and (3) training is documented.

WHEN WILL THE AUDIT OCCUR?

Once again, *when* an audit is to occur may vary, depending on organizational or other issues within the district or school, those audited, and the auditor. Audits can be performed annually, semiannually, continuously, etc. It is recommended that a school district (and the corresponding school) audits be done at least once a year. One possible timing arrangement would be to have an independent outside auditor do an audit annually and have an internal auditor conduct an audit on a semiannual basis.

CREATING/OBTAINING AUDITING MATERIALS

It is important that auditing materials reflect information needed by the district and/or school. A simple spreadsheet, workbook page, or table can be employed to obtain such data. Remember information needed by each district or school—for example, how the term "appropriate employee" is defined. Therefore one distinct form may not be applicable to all districts or schools. Each educational entity may create/re-create its own based on the information provided in this chapter. That having been said, sample forms (see Figures 6.3 and 6.4), as well as an explanation of what each audit statement means, are provided in the following sections.

CLARIFYING THE DISTRICT LEVEL AUDIT SHEET

In order to more clearly demonstrate how to conduct a district level copyright compliance audit for utmost effectiveness, we now go through each item on the sample sheet shown in Figure 6.3. This is to add clarity to the sorts of questions that are asked and of whom in order to ensure that the audit truly reflects how well the policy is being followed.

Let's first examine the district audit sheets line by line:

1. **A district copyright compliance policy has been established.**
   Given this audit statement, the auditor should ask to see a copy of the school copyright policy. Said policy should be written and readily available.

2. **The district level copyright compliance policy is reviewed on an annual basis to ensure currency.**
   Here, the auditor asks to see written documentation that the policy is reviewed. This documentation should include the date of the review and the signature of the reviewer. The auditor should also assess the policy to ensure that it actually does comply with current copyright law.

3. **The copyright compliance policy has been communicated to all appropriate district employees, including district administrators, technology coordinators, and librarians.**
   For statement three, the auditor asks to see written documentation that the policy meetings were held and that a record of those in attendance was kept. The auditor should also randomly select some of the appropriate district employees (teachers, librarians, and others) and ask them if they recall being informed of the district copyright compliance policy.

4. **Copyright compliance policy training is provided to all appropriate district employees on a regular basis.**
   Given this statement, the auditor asks to see a copy of the lesson plan (outline) that was used by the trainer.

District Level			Date
AUDIT STATEMENTS	YES	NO	ACTION REQUIRED
1. A district level copyright compliance policy has been established.			
2. The district level copyright compliance policy is reviewed on an annual basis to ensure currency.			
3. The copyright compliance policy has been communicated to all appropriate district employees, including district administrators, technology coordinators, and librarians.			
4. Copyright compliance policy training is provided to all appropriate district employees on a regular basis.			
5. Copyright compliance policy training is provided to all appropriate new district employees as part of their initial orientation.			
6. All district copyright compliance policy training is documented.			
7. A district copyright "expert" has been established. District employees are aware of the identity of this person.			
8. The copyright "expert" has been trained on and is current in copyright law as it pertains to all areas of focus within the district.			
9. The district copyright compliance audit is conducted on a regular basis. Results of the audit are communicated to appropriate district personnel.			
10. Follow-up district action items are completed in a timely manner and completion is documented.			

Figure 6.3. District Level Copyright Compliance Audit Sheet (Sample)

The auditor should also ask to see written documentation that the training took place, that it takes place on the frequency outlined in the policies and procedures, and that the district keeps a record of those in attendance as well as the dates these individuals were trained. The auditor also needs to randomly select some of the appropriate district employees and ask them if they recall being trained on the policy other than the initial training.

5. **Copyright compliance policy training is provided to all appropriate new district employees as part of their initial orientation.**

   For this item, the auditor asks to see a copy of the lesson plan (outline) used for new employee orientation in order to ensure that the copyright compliance policy is included. The auditor needs to see written documentation of dates and attendees for the training. In addition, the auditor should randomly select several employees hired since the last audit and ask them if they recall being informed of the district copyright compliance policy during their initial orientation.

6. **All district copyright compliance policy training is documented.**

   The auditor will be checking for proper documentation as part of the previous items. However, this statement serves as a general reminder for the auditor and reinforces the need for proper documentation of training.

7. **A district copyright "expert" has been established. District employees are aware of the identity of this person.**

   Here, the auditor meets the district "expert" and determines that this individual is aware that he or she is the "expert." Additionally, the auditor should also randomly select several other district employees and ask them if they know who the district "expert" is.

8. **The copyright "expert" has been trained on and is current in copyright law as it pertains to all areas of focus within the district.**

   For this item, the auditor asks the "expert" when he or she was trained and by whom. The auditor should also ask to see any documentation (certificate of training completion, transcripts, etc.) that the "expert" is able to provide in order to determine if he or she is adequately trained and current in school copyright issues.

9. **The district copyright compliance audit is conducted on a regular basis. Results of the audit are communicated to appropriate district personnel.**

   For statement nine, the auditor needs to ask to see copies of previous district audits to ensure that these appraisals were performed at the prescribed frequency and that the results were communicated to the district stakeholders.

10. **Follow-up district action items are completed in a timely manner and completion is documented.**

    At this point, the auditor asks to see documentation that action items were truly completed—for example, a report that includes the date of completion and who completed the items. The auditor should also randomly select a few previous action items and ensure that they were also actually completed.

CLARIFYING THE SCHOOL/BUILDING LEVEL AUDIT SHEET

In order to more clearly demonstrate how to conduct a school level copyright compliance audit for utmost effectiveness, we now go through each item on the sample sheet shown previously. As with the district audit sheet, this discussion adds clarity to the sorts of questions that are asked and of whom in order to ensure that the audit truly reflects how well the policy is being followed.

Now let's examine the school audit sheets line by line:

1. **The district copyright compliance policy has been communicated to all building level employees, including teachers, technology specialists, school library media specialists, and staff.**

   For this item, the auditor asks to see written documentation that the policy meetings were held and that a record of those in attendance was kept. The auditor should also randomly select some of the appropriate school employees (teachers, librarians, and others) and ask them if they recall being informed of the district copyright compliance policy.

2. **The district copyright compliance policy has been posted in appropriate school building areas (copy machines, school library media center, staff bulletin boards, etc.).**

   For this statement, the auditor needs to observe the selected school building areas (states in statement two)

School/Building Level			Date
AUDIT STATEMENTS	YES	NO	ACTION REQUIRED
1. The district copyright compliance policy has been communicated to all building level employees, including teachers, technology specialists, school library media specialists, and staff.			
2. The district copyright compliance policy has been posted in appropriate school building areas (copy machines, school library media center, staff bulletin boards, etc.).			
3. District copyright compliance policy training is provided to all building employees at least annually.			
4. District copyright compliance policy training is provided to all new building employees as part of their initial orientation.			
5. District copyright compliance policy training is provided to all students as part of the regular school curriculum.			
6. All district copyright compliance policy training, no matter who is trained, is documented.			
7. A school copyright "expert" has been determined and all school personnel and students are aware of this person's identity.			
8. The school copyright "expert" has been trained and is current on copyright law as it applies to the school.			
9. The school copyright "expert" or another designated building person maintains a current list of licenses and other contractual agreements made by the school to various software, database, etc., companies.			

Figure 6.4. School/Building Level Copyright Compliance Audit Sheet (Sample)

School/Building Level			Date
AUDIT STATEMENTS	YES	NO	ACTION REQUIRED
10. The school copyright "expert" maintains a list of copyright issues that have arisen and the resolution of those issues.			
11. A building copyright compliance audit is conducted at least annually and results are communicated to appropriate school personnel (for example, school administrators, technology specialists, school library media specialists, teachers, etc.).			
12. Follow-up actions are completed in a timely manner and completion is documented.			

Figure 6.4. School/Building Level Copyright Compliance Audit Sheet (Sample) (Continued)

during the audit and confirm that the policy is posted and clearly visible to all.

3. **District copyright compliance policy training is provided to all building employees at least annually.**
Here, the auditor asks to see a copy of the lesson plan (outline) that was used by the trainer. The auditor then additionally asks to see written documentation that the training took place, including a record of those in attendance and the training dates. The auditor should also randomly select several appropriate school employees and ask them if they recall being trained on the policy other than the initial training.

4. **District copyright compliance policy training is provided to all new building employees as part of their initial orientation.**
For this item, the auditor asks to see a copy of the lesson plan (outline) used for new employee orientation and ensure that the copyright compliance policy is included. The auditor also needs to see written documentation of this orientation training, including training dates and the attendees. In addition, the auditor should randomly select several employees hired since the last audit and ask them if they recall being informed of the district copyright compliance policy during their initial orientation.

5. **District copyright compliance policy training is provided to all students as part of the regular school curriculum.**

   This is an important statement; it demonstrates that copyright compliance is also vital to the school's students. Here, the auditor asks to see a copy of the lesson plan(s) used to teach the students. To ensure that copyright lessons are part of the normal school curriculum, the auditor also needs to randomly select several students and ask them if they recall learning about the district copyright compliance policy.

6. **All district copyright compliance policy training, no matter who is trained, is documented.**

   The auditor will be checking for proper documentation as part of the previous items. However, this item serves as a general reminder for the auditor as well as reinforcing the need for proper documentation of training.

7. **A school copyright "expert" has been determined and all school personnel and students are aware of this person's identity.**

   For this item, the auditor should ask to meet the school "expert" and determine that he or she is aware that he or she is the "expert." The auditor should also randomly select several other school employees and students and ask them if they know who the district "expert" is.

8. **The school copyright "expert" has been trained and is current on copyright law as it applies to the school.**
   For this item, it is imperative that the auditor ask the "expert" when he or she was trained and by whom. The auditor should also ask to see any documentation (certificate of training completion, transcripts, etc.) that proves the "expert" is adequately trained and up to date.

9. **The school copyright "expert" or another designated building person maintains a current list of licenses and other contractual agreements made by the school to various software, database, etc., companies.**
   Given statement nine, the auditor should ask to see a copy of the list of current licenses and agreements made by the school.

10. **The school copyright "expert" maintains a list of copyright issues that have arisen and the resolution of those issues.**
    For this item, the auditor asks to see the list of school copyright issues. The auditor also needs to (1) randomly

select a resolved issue or two and ascertain that the resolution complies with current copyright law and (2) inquire about the current status of any unresolved issues.

11. **A building copyright compliance audit is conducted at least annually and results are communicated to appropriate school personnel (for example, school administrators, technology specialists, school library media specialists, teachers, etc.).**
Here, the auditor asks to see copies of previous school audits. The auditor also needs to see a record that these audits were conducted on a prescribed frequency and that the results were communicated to the stakeholders (administration, faculty, and others).

12. **Follow-up actions are completed in a timely manner and completion is documented.**
For this item, the auditor asks to see documentation that action items were actually completed. Such documentation should include the date of completion and who completed these actions. Additionally, the auditor also needs to randomly select a few of the previous action items in order to determine that they were completed as well.

The two sample audit sheets in this chapter represent the more common criteria that a district (Figure 6.3) and school (Figure 6.4) would need in order to determine if they had obtained, or were working toward, copyright compliancy. Such statements as those found in these sheets can be used in written format in a survey or questionnaire or verbally in individual or focus group interviews. The recommended format of the audit is that which is most comfortable for those being audited, as long as the purpose of the audit is not compromised.

Next is discussed the conducting of the audit.

CONDUCTING THE AUDIT

The audit is conducted:

1. for the district and/or the schools within the district;
2. by an external or internal auditor or by a team of auditors, including at least one external and one internal member;

3. with those who have the most "buy-in" in copyright compliancy (in this case district administrators and media and technology personnel and/or building administrators, technology coordinators, school library media specialists, teachers, and staff);
4. using a survey or individual or focus group interviews;
5. in the district office as well as the individual schools;
6. at a specific time, to be determined by the district and those conducting the audit.[2]

Remember, it is important to make sure that all materials needed for an audit are readily available to the auditor at the beginning of the audit.

CONCLUSION

This chapter covers (1) the audit process, (2) the audit meetings, (3) auditing procedures, (4) examples of criteria needed in auditing materials as well as sample audit sheets, (5) auditors, and (6) conducting an audit. As the "go-to" person introduced at the beginning of this chapter, you now have the information you need to inform your teachers of the audit process. In addition, you now have specific information on how to perform an audit, should the district and/or the school decide to utilize internal auditors. Once the audit is over, we turn to feedback and who is in charge of responding to it. Chapter 7 addresses these topics.

NOTES

1. The "Big6" is an information-seeking process used by middle and high school teachers and librarians to inform their students' researching/problem-solving skills. It is composed of six distinct steps: (1) task definition, (2) information-seeking strategies, (3) location and access, (4) use of information, (5) synthesis, and (6) evaluation (Bennett, 2007).
2. Audit feedback informational support for this chapter comes from personal interviews with Thomas W. Butler, Manufacturing, Plant Engineering and Maintenance Management Consultant. Butler has been trained to conduct International Organization for Standardization (ISO) audits for commercial and manufacturing environments and has also participated in internal quality audits for several manufacturing

companies, including Oscar Mayer Foods Corporation, Kraft Foods Incorporated, and OSI Food Company.

REFERENCES

Bennett, Blythe. 2007. "Why Do We Use the Big6™? . . . It All Points to FOCUS!" Syracuse, NY: Syracuse University. Available: www .big6.com/showarticle.php?id=274 (accessed February 27, 2008).

Encarta World English Dictionary. 1999. s.v. "Audit." Redmond, WA: Microsoft Corporation.

7 FEEDBACK AND CONCLUSION

INTRODUCTION

Let's imagine that you, a middle school principal, have been a driving force, not only in your school's participation in proactive copyright compliance but also in your district's positive stance with this issue. Additionally, you encouraged all faculty and staff to comply with auditing requirements. Now you find that you and those you have been working with want to "put away" all thoughts and activities dealing with schools and copyright and get on with your lives. Should this happen?

Once you have gone through all of the work of developing district copyright compliance policies and procedures, identifying the key personnel, conducting the training, and initiating the audit process for both the district and participating schools within it, the natural tendency is to take a deep breath, relax, and move on to something else. This is okay; you deserve it. However, in order to ensure that the copyright compliance process continues and remains current, the policies and procedures need to be living documents. Fortunately, the copyright compliance process itself, specifically the audit process, can provide this. If done correctly, the audit process will not only ensure that the policies and procedures remain "alive" but it will also provide you the opportunity to continually improve the entire process. In this chapter, we examine how the audit process can do this for you.

A WORD ABOUT PURPOSE AND INTENT

At this point we would do well to remember that the purpose of establishing a district/school copyright compliance process is to ensure that you are doing everything you can to comply with copyright law. While there is probably no way to be absolutely certain that your district or school will never find itself infringing on someone's copyright ownership, it would seem to make sense that such occurrences would be far less likely the more thorough you are in establishing, following, and keeping your compliance policies and procedures current.

Also, while you may find yourself at odds with copyright law at some point despite your best efforts, it seems fitting that anyone charged with making a judgment or resolution in a copyright compliance dispute would take the intent of the parties into account. By having established policies and procedures and being proactive in ensuring that you follow them, you are establishing that your clear intent is to comply with the law.

In Figure 7.1 the copyright compliance process flowchart informs us of this last point in the process: provide feedback for continuous improvement of the process.

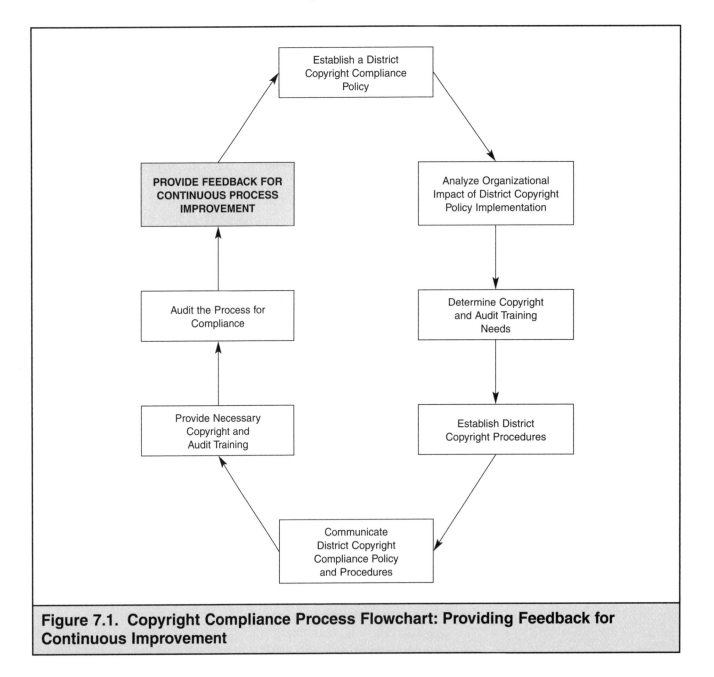

Figure 7.1. Copyright Compliance Process Flowchart: Providing Feedback for Continuous Improvement

FEEDBACK

Several stages of the audit process provide feedback. The audit is really "a picture in time" of how your copyright compliance process is working. In addition, it can be used as a springboard for continuous improvement of your existing process.

We now discuss the three stages of the audit process that provide feedback and offer hypothetical examples of how such feedback can be used to improve your district and/or school copyright compliance process.

AUDIT STAGES THAT PROVIDE FEEDBACK

- **Immediate feedback:** This first type of feedback is provided during the audit interview itself. For example, let's assume that an auditor asks to see a copy of the district copyright compliance policy at step one of the district audit and, for some reason, no one is able to find it. The auditor would immediately make the observation that the document, which is not accessible, should be readily available at all times.

- **Audit-closing meeting:** Provided verbally by the auditor as the last step of the audit process, this is the second kind of feedback. At the audit-closing meeting, the auditor goes over the results of the audit with all appropriate personnel. He or she then provides specific details of any deficiencies found. In addition, the auditor may offer suggestions as to how to improve something that is already taking place. For example, let's assume that the auditor establishes that there were handwritten records of the copyright policy training at steps three and six of the school audit. However, these records were somewhat hard to read and poorly organized. The auditor might suggest that the records be kept electronically so that they could be more easily maintained and retrieved.

- **Final report:** The auditor provides the final report to all stakeholders in writing. (It is important that auditors supply written documentation of their findings. This ensures that the district/school has a copy of the audit results as well as a written means to make recommended follow-up actions.) Nothing in the final report should come as a surprise to those who are being audited. Any deficiencies or required action items should have already been communicated orally at the closing meeting. It is good practice to inform those you are working with verbally as well as in writing. However, the auditor can use the final report to expand on any recommendations for improvement that he or she might have. For example, let's assume that the high school library media specialist has been identified as the school's "expert," and the auditor determines that this person has been well trained. However, the auditor is aware that several changes in copyright law have taken place since the librarian received his or her training, thus the auditor might suggest in the final report that the "expert" be scheduled for additional instruction on the changes to the law.

OTHER OPPORTUNITIES FOR FEEDBACK

While the audit section of the copyright compliance process is specifically designed to provide feedback about the complete course of action for either the district or the school, there are several other points that have the potential for process improvement. In general, these would be any time in the process that communication is taking place. For example, this would include initial meetings, the compliance training, and/or new employee training. In all of these cases, the meeting/training facilitator should take the opportunity to solicit feedback from the participants (trainees) as to the content and quality of the meeting/training sessions. This feedback can then be used to improve these sessions.

A WORD ABOUT AUDITORS AND FEEDBACK

Since a primary purpose of the process audits is to offer feedback to (1) ensure compliance and (2) provide opportunities for continuous improvement, the selection of auditors is critical to the effectiveness of this criticism/advice. With this in mind, I suggest that auditors be placed in positions where they audit people and processes other than their own. Because auditors function as an "extra set of eyes," it is difficult for them to be unbiased if they are working with specific individuals or on particular processes on a day-to-day basis. In such cases, there may be a tendency to ignore non-copyright-compliant issues or activities since these may happen every day and appear normal or because the auditor may be unaware of other ways of doing things.[1]

While the use of an external auditor would certainly ensure that the district and/or school have that "outside observer," the same thing could be accomplished while still relying on internal district personnel to conduct the audits. Examples of this might include using a district administrator to audit the high school, high school technology coordinator to audit middle and elementary schools, etc.

CONCLUSION

Remember the beginning of this chapter? You, a middle school principal, have been very active, not only in your school's participation in proactive copyright compliance but also in your district's positive stance with this issue. You have listened to the auditor's accounts, read the feedback reports, and discussed with the other stakeholders what needs to be accomplished, given these reports. Are you done? Well, as can be seen, the answer is that the copyright compliance process is alive, ongoing. In order for compliancy, the proactive copyright compliance process needs to be a continuing part of your school district's programmatic goals and, moreover, a part of its ethical mission.[2]

In this chapter we have closed the copyright compliance process loop. Including a feedback step in the process ensures that your policies and procedures are "living" documents and that your process continues to improve over time. Maintaining copyright compliance—whether you are working on the district-wide level, in an individual school, in a library, technology center, or classroom—remains the same: a living, breathing subject. Your intent to act in accordance with copyright law is now clear. "Go forth and conquer..." (Tennyson, 1898: 459).

NOTES

1. Audit feedback informational support for this chapter comes from personal interviews with Thomas W. Butler, Manufacturing, Plant Engineering and Maintenance Management Consultant. Butler has been trained to conduct International Organization for Standardization (ISO) audits for commercial and manufacturing environments and has also participated in internal quality audits for several manufacturing companies, including Oscar Mayer Foods Corporation, Kraft Foods Incorporated, and OSI Food Company.
2. Please refer to the discussion of law and ethics in Chapter 2.

REFERENCE

Tennyson, A. 1898. *The Works of Alfred Lord Tennyson Poet Laureate.* New York: The Macmillan Company.

COMPLIANCE
TOOLBOX

TOOL **I** # SAMPLE COPYRIGHT COMPLIANCE TRAINING MATERIALS

Tool I holds the following examples of copyright compliance training materials: External Expert Initial Meeting Proposal: Proactive Copyright Compliance, Copyright Question and Answer Presentation, Generic Copyright Compliance Training Syllabus, Generic Discussion Questions for School District Copyright Compliance Trainees, and Generic Training Ideas.

EXTERNAL EXPERT INITIAL MEETING PROPOSAL: PROACTIVE COPYRIGHT COMPLIANCE

PROPOSAL PURPOSE

To discover what a school district serious about copyright law needs to have in place in order to be copyright compliant.

DISTRICT AT PRESENT

Policy

School district has a copyright policy in place.

Procedures

Copyright compliance process and procedures do not exist.

Training

Formal copyright training does not exist.

Audit

Formal copyright auditing procedures do not exist.

INITIAL MEETING

The initial meeting is to discuss a proposed process to ensure copyright compliance within _____ School District. Discussion will include input from district participants, focus on the process itself, look at how the proposed process will affect _____ School District, and initiate actions required to implement the process. To be generated at this meeting: *who* communicates the policy, *how* is the policy communicated, *to whom* is the policy communicated, *who* will do the audits, *when* will auditing occur, *who* will be accountable and for *what*, and more as appropriate to meeting attendees and their needs.

MATERIALS TO BE PROVIDED BY EXTERNAL EXPERT

- **Proposed process flowcharts**. These will include information on the organizational impact and the role of the district administrators and others in implementing the process.
- **Sample training materials and activities**. These will address the training needs identified during the initial meeting.
- **Sample auditing materials and activities**. These are provided as examples to be used to ensure policy compliance.
- **Proposed follow-up activities**.

TIME

Estimate of time for the initial meeting is two hours: the first hour for presentation/discussion of the proposed process and the second hour for general copyright discussion/Q&A.

FACILITATOR'S FEE

Preparation time, meeting time, and mileage: $_____.

PROACTIVE COPYRIGHT COMPLIANCE PRESENTATION

This is presented in outline form. It could also be generated using presentation software.

I. The Question

What does a school district, serious about copyright law, need to have in place in order to be copyright compliant?

II. What Is Needed

  A. Copyright policy

  B. Procedures for copyright compliance process

  C. Formal copyright training

  D. Formal copyright auditing

III. Copyright Compliance Procedures

  A. Establish copyright compliance policy

  B. Establish copyright compliance procedures

  C. Communicate the policy

  D. Provide necessary training and documentation

  E. Audit the process

  F. Provide feedback

IV. The Policy

  A. Establish the policy

    1. Ask: What should be included in the copyright policy?

    2. Ask: Who will check to ensure that all bases are covered?

  B. Communicate the policy

    1. Who will communicate the policy?

      a. District staff?

      b. School administrators?

      c. Individual school faculty and staff?

    2. How will the policy be communicated?

      a. Teachers' meetings

      b. Binders

      c. School intranet

    3. To whom is the policy communicated?

      a. Administrators

      b. Teachers

      c. Librarians

      d. Technology and curriculum coordinators

      e. Students

      f. Others

V. The Training

  A. Who to train

    1. District level personnel

    2. Administrators

    3. All librarians and technology coordinators

    4. All faculty and staff

    5. Students

  B. What to train

    1. Copyright for public schools

    2. Copyright for teachers and administrators

    3. Copyright for students

          4. Compliance audit procedures
      C. How to train
          1. Outside training resources
          2. Internal trainers
      D. Sample training materials
          1. Books
          2. Articles
          3. Copyright classes
          4. Copyright workshops
          5. Selected resources handout
  VI. The Audit
      A. Audit process
      B. Audit procedures
      C. Why do we audit?
          1. To document compliance
          2. To show good intentions
          3. To help ensure continuous improvement
          4. Other
      D. How will we audit?
          1. Surveys
          2. Focus groups
          3. Other
          4. Sample audit questions
      E. Who will conduct the audits?
          1. Outside auditors
          2. Internal auditors
          3. Combination of the two
      F. When will we audit?
          1. Continuously
          2. Annually
          3. When needed
 VII. Feedback
      A. Use audit results to provide feedback/improve process
      B. How? Documentation.
      C. When? End of year; continuously.
VIII. Where Do We Go from Here?
      A. Small group work
      B. Discussion with administrators

BIBLIOGRAPHY

Butler, Rebecca P. 2004. *Copyright for Teachers and Librarians*. New
    York: Neal-Schuman.
United States Constitution. Article 1. Section 8.
United States Copyright Law. 1976–Present.

COPYRIGHT QUESTION AND ANSWER PRESENTATION

This is presented in outline form. It could also be generated using presentation software. Answers to sample school copyright questions in this presentation are found, as identified after each question, in Butler, Rebecca P., 2004, *Copyright for Teachers and Librarians*, New York: Neal-Schuman.

 I. Media That Can Be Copyright Protected
  A. Those things from a creative mind
 II. Ways to Borrow/Copy Legally
  A. Law
   1. Fair use
   2. Public domain
   3. Permission
  B. Guidelines
 III. Types of Infringement
  A. Direct
  B. Contributory
  C. Vicarious
 IV. Sample School Copyright Questions
  A. Can we legally copy book cover images from the Internet and put them on our library's homepage? (Butler, 2004: 70–71)
  B. Can we send copies of school software home with students so that they might finish a homework assignment? (Butler, 2004: 134–135)
  C. Can we use an entertainment video or DVD in the classroom? (Butler, 2004: 88, 92)
  D. Can our school cheerleaders use popular music for their routines? (Butler, 2004: 152–153)
 V. Questions?

BIBLIOGRAPHY

Butler, Rebecca P. 2004. *Copyright for Teachers and Librarians*. New York: Neal-Schuman.
United States Constitution. Article 1. Section 8.
United States Copyright Law. 1976–Present.

GENERIC COPYRIGHT COMPLIANCE TRAINING SYLLABUS

DESCRIPTION

Introduction to copyright law as needed for District _____ school personnel copyright compliance.

OBJECTIVES

Following training, activities, discussion, etc., school personnel will be able to do the following:

1. Define copyright law in terms of District _____ needs
2. Identify copyright issues of concern and react to them in a timely manner
3. Recognize an infringement and determine to whom to report it
4. Read and discuss copyright support materials
5. Explain the "fair use doctrine" and the four criteria that determine "fair use"
6. Interpret copyright restrictions in terms of various print and non-print media
7. Demonstrate a working knowledge of equipment and resources within the legal/copyright restrictions
8. Obtain permission from owners of copyrighted materials
9. Teach/train the students of District _____ about copyright law

COURSE TOPICS

Copyright and

- World Wide Web
- Computer Software
- Videos, CDs, and DVDs
- Audio
- Sheet music

- Print materials
- Other countries
- Teaching
- Obtaining permission
- Piracy
- Plagiarism
- Other (as is pertinent to each particular school district)

BIBLIOGRAPHY

Butler, Rebecca P. 2004. *Copyright for Teachers and Librarians*. New York: Neal-Schuman. Another up-to-date book on copyright for the K–12 school environment.
Other assigned readings as appropriate.

COURSE ACTIVITIES

1. Lectures and demonstrations by the instructor
2. Reading assignments
3. Discussion
4. Written assignments
5. Oral presentations
6. Possible guest speakers

TRAINING REQUIREMENTS

1. Attendance/participation
2. Assignments as appropriate

SELECTED BIBLIOGRAPHY

Bruwelheide, Janet H. 1995. *The Copyright Primer for Librarians and Educators*, Second Edition. Chicago, IL: American Library Association.
Butler, Rebecca P. 2003. "Copyright Law and Organizing the Internet." *Library Trends* 52, no. 2: 307–317.
Crewes, Kenneth D. 2000. *Copyright Essentials for Librarians and Educators*. Chicago, IL: American Library Association.

Hoffmann, Gretchen McCord. 2001. *Copyright in Cyberspace Questions and Answers for Librarians*. New York: Neal-Schuman Publishers.

Lipinski, Tomas A. (Ed.). 2002. *Libraries, Museums, and Archives: Legal Issues and Ethical Challanges in the New Information Era*. Lanham, MD: Scarecrow Press.

Rose, Mark. 1993. *Authors and Owners: The Invention of Copyright*. Cambridge, MA: Harvard University Press.

Simpson, Carol Mann. 2001. *Copyright for Schools: A Practical Guide*, Third Edition. Worthington, OH: Linworth Publishing.

Talab, R. S. 1999. *Common Sense Copyright: A Guide for Educators and Librarians*, Second Edition. Jefferson, NC: McFarland and Co.

Torrans, Lee Ann. 2003. *Law for K–12 Libraries and Librarians*. Westport, CT: Libraries Unlimited.

United States Constitution. Article 1. Section 8.

United States Copyright Law. 1976-Present.

U.S. Copyright Office. 2006. "Searching by the U.S. Copyright Office." Available: www.loc.gov/copyright/circs/circ22.html#searching.

GENERIC DISCUSSION QUESTIONS FOR SCHOOL DISTRICT COPYRIGHT COMPLIANCE TRAINEES

These questions are samples of what will be asked of District _____ copyright compliance training participants. These will be answered during the training session(s) and/or used to promote reflection.

1. What do you want out of copyright compliance training?

2. How will this help you in your work in District _____?

3. What is intellectual property? Copyright?

4. What is the relationship between copyright and plagiarism?

5. How do copyright laws affect you personally? In your work in District _____?

6. Have you ever violated copyright laws in your work? Personal life? What were the reasons? What were the results?

7. Have you ever approached a copyright holder for permission? How helpful was that person or company?

8. What changes would you like to see in copyright law?

9. Should links (Internet) be copyrighted?

10. What can't be copyright protected?

11. How important to learning is the use of copyrighted material in the classroom?

12. What kinds of copyrighted materials do you spend the most money on? (This question would be especially important to those who purchase materials as part of their day-to-day employment, such as school library media specialists and similar school/district personnel.)

13. How much freedom should teachers and students have to reproduce for educational purposes?

14. Should teachers and/or students be paid if their work is distributed on networks? Should they be asked if they want their material up on a digital network?

15. How do we politely inform others (our students, fellow teachers, administrators, etc.) that they are in copyright violation?

16. How do we deal with administrators and fellow workers who ask us to infringe on an owner's copyright?

17. Who owns our work? Our students' work?

18. What is the Digital Millennium Copyright Act (DMCA)? Why is it important to us in K–12 education?

19. Should we register works if they are copyright protected anyway?

20. Is copying someone's e-mail a copyright violation?

21. How can we work within copyright law so that it is our friend?

22. Is it okay to use pirated videos and software if these items come from another country?

23. How do we work within a law that requires the user to police himself or herself?

GENERIC TRAINING IDEAS

PRESENTATION/LECTURE/DISCUSSION SUBJECTS

1. Introduction to Intellectual Property

2. Copyright in the Public School Setting (General Overview): Defined, Statutory Exemptions, Public Domain,

Guidelines, Getting Permission, Clearinghouses, Licenses, Formats, International Issues, and more

3. Copyright subjects of specific interest to the various special groups (stakeholders) to be trained—for example, specific parts of the copyright law, copyright and particular formats of materials, etc.

4. Copyright Review of #2 or #3

5. Ethics Versus the Law

ACTIVITIES

Copyright Observation

Copyright infringement happens every day, either intentionally or unintentionally. Take a half hour and observe (unobtrusively) in an area where copyright may be infringed on: near a photocopy machine, by a computer, in your classroom or library, in the teachers' lounge, etc. Take notes. You will report orally in our next training session on what you have observed.

Permission Activity

Using a variety of sources (which may include but are not limited to the U.S. Copyright Office, the Internet, print and nonprint sources), compile information discussing how you would go about obtaining permission to copy something needed for your classroom or work assignment or find a real-life example of something that you need permission to use in your work. Work through how to obtain this permission and/or actually obtain permission to use the item. Permission example ideas include getting permission for a high school class to put on a production of a particular play, use of a specific video or DVD for a middle school student organization, obtaining permission to use a popular song as part of a cheerleading performance, and obtaining permission to use a cartoon on an elementary school Web page. You need to document the following for this activity: your steps to obtaining permission; how you would obtain copyright owner contact information; one-three agencies, clearinghouses, or other organizations that can help you find the copyright owner; and finding/creating a sample permission letter, written to your specific permission request. Participants can do this either during a training session or at another time and report back in their next training session.

Copyright Article

Find an article on copyright. The sky is the limit here—it can be on any aspect of copyright that you find interesting or important. You may find the article in print sources or on the Internet. Read the article. Bring the article to the next training session. Report on orally in large group. (I have found that this activity encourages participants to look for something that they are interested in, thus finding that copyright issues can affect them personally, not just "others.")

Copyright Lessons for _____ School Students

After trainer-led discussion on teaching copyright to students and seeing examples of student-level copyright information on the Web, either working with a partner or by yourself, surf the Web for examples of copyright lessons that you might use with your students. Briefly read through and consider at least three sites. Share these in the training session with other participants.

SAMPLE AUDIT SCENARIO, AUDIT, AND FINAL REPORT

AUDIT SCENARIO

You are the school library media specialist at Thomas Jefferson High School in Illinois district 1234. As part of your duties, you are also a copyright compliance auditor for the district. You have scheduled an annual compliance audit at Abraham Lincoln Middle School for November 19, 2008. (You make it a habit to schedule compliance audits at least a week before the audit occurs in order to make sure that all those to be audited are ready and not surprised by your visit.)

At 7:30 a.m., you arrive at the middle school and conduct an opening meeting with the principal, Ms. White; the school library media specialist, Mr. Brown; the technology specialist, Mr. Green; and several other teachers and staff. At that meeting, you explain the purpose of the audit and schedule time with key faculty and staff for later in the day. You also set 4:00 p.m. as the time for a closing meeting.

After the early morning meeting, you tour the school with the principal in order to get familiar with the location of the library, technology center, copy center, etc. Next, during the course of the day, you meet at scheduled times with key personnel in order to answer the questions on the audit checklist. You also spend time on your own observing in the school.

While on your own, you stop and randomly ask faculty, staff, and students questions such as:

1. Are you familiar with the District Copyright Compliance Policy?

2. Have you been trained on the policy?

3. Do you know where to find a copy of the policy?

4. Who would you go to if you had a copyright compliance issue?

5. Have you had any copyright compliance issues? How were they resolved?

As the day passes, you find that the school, in general, does a very good job of complying with the district's policy. You do, however, discover several issues that you record on the audit checklist. These are the following:

1. There is a new remote copy center located in the music area of the school. The district compliance policy is not posted in that area. You mention this to the band teacher and she says that she will post a copy immediately. You later go back through the area and notice that a copy of the policy has, indeed, been posted.

2. You are introduced to a substitute English teacher who is filling in for the semester while the regular teacher is off on a family medical leave. You ask him if he has been trained on the district's copyright compliance policy and discover that he has not. As you note this on the audit checklist, you realize that the training of substitutes is probably an issue for most schools in the district and should be addressed with an update of the copyright policy.

3. During your meeting with the school library media (SLM) specialist (who is also the school's "go-to" person), you ask to see the documentation that copyright compliance training has taken place. He produces a sign-up sheet for the training. While it appears to be complete, you notice that the date the training occurred does not appear on the sheet.

4. Last, during your meeting with the SLM you discover that, although he has attended external copyright training, it has been two years since the training occurred. You are aware that new changes in the law regarding electronic media have just been implemented.

At 4:00 p.m. you once again meet with the key school personnel for a closing meeting. At that time you thank them for their hospitality and cooperation. You then review the audit results and address all of the specific items that you found along with your recommendations for correcting them. You ask for any questions about the results. At the close of the meeting, you advise the group that a formal written report will be coming to them within the next week and that this report will also be sent to the district superintendent. You make it clear that nothing will appear in the final report that you haven't already addressed at the meeting.

Over the next few days, you complete your written audit report and send copies to the district and the school.

COPYRIGHT COMPLIANCE AUDIT

In this section, the reader will find a sample copy of the audit checklist for the previous audit scenario, and in the next section a sample final report. Please note that in this case, the audit generated direct feedback for the school. In addition, in accordance with the feedback step in the copyright compliance process, it also generated feedback for the district to improve the process (specifically, the need to address how to ensure that substitute teachers receive the necessary training).

SCHOOL DISTRICT: Illinois District 1234			SCHOOL: Lincoln Middle School DATE: _____
School Level	**Yes**	**No**	**Action Required**
1. The district copyright compliance policy has been communicated to all appropriate employees, including teachers and school library media specialists.	X		
2. The district copyright compliance policy is posted in appropriate areas (copy machines, school library media center, staff bulletin boards, etc.)		X	Remote copy center in music area needs policy posted.
3. Training on the policy is provided to all employees at least annually.	X		
4. Training on the policy is provided to all new employees as part of their initial orientation.		X	Extended term English substitute needs to be trained. District policy update required.
5. Training on the policy is provided for all students as part of the regular school curriculum.	X		
6. There is documentation that the appropriate training on the policy has been conducted.	X		List of those trained exists; however, the date of training needs to be recorded.

Figure II.1. Copyright Compliance Audit

School Level	Yes	No	Action Required
7. A school copyright "go-to" person has been established and the school staff is aware of who this person is.	X		
8. The "go-to" person has been trained and is current on copyright law as it applies to the school.		X	Need to schedule update training. New changes in the law have occurred.
9. The "go-to" person maintains a log of copyright issues that have arisen and the resolution of those issues.	X		
10. A compliance audit is conducted at least annually, and the results are communicated to the stakeholders.	X		
11. Follow-up action items are completed in a timely manner and completion is documented.	X		

Figure II.1. Copyright Compliance Audit *(Continued)*

FINAL REPORT

Thomas Jefferson High School
Illinois School District 1234
Prairie City, Illinois

November 26, 2008

TO: Ms. A. White, Principal, Lincoln Middle School

     Mr. B. Brown, School Library Media Specialist, Lincoln Middle School

     Mr. C. Green, Technology Specialist, Lincoln Middle School

     Dr. D. Black, Superintendent, Illinois School District 1234

FROM: Rebecca P. Butler, School Library Media Specialist, Jefferson High School

SUBJECT: Copyright Compliance Audit—Final Report

OVERVIEW

On November 19, 2008, I conducted a copyright compliance audit at Lincoln Middle School. I met with Ms. White, Mr. Brown, Mr. Green, and several other members of the faculty and staff at the school. The audit consisted of an opening meeting, a tour of the school, the actual audit, and a closing meeting.

In general, the school is doing a very good job of complying with both the District Copyright Compliance Policy and copyright law as it applies there. The faculty and staff are aware of the policy and take it seriously. There have been copyright questions within the past year. In each case, the question was brought to Mr. Brown and he was able to resolve it. In addition, he keeps a very thorough log of these issues and their resolution. It is clear that it is the intent of this school to be copyright compliant.

During the course of the audit, I did find several minor issues that I noted on the audit checklist (attached). These issues were fully discussed at the closing meeting on the day of the audit and, in some cases, have already been resolved.

I again want to thank Ms. White and her entire staff for the courtesy and cooperation they showed me during the course of this audit.

SPECIFIC ISSUES AND RECOMMENDATIONS

1. There is a new remote copy center in the music area of the school. I noticed that a copy of the district compliance policy was not posted in this area even though it was posted in all other copy areas. I brought this to the attention of the band director who immediately corrected the situation.

2. The school has employed a substitute teacher in the English department for the entire semester while the regular teacher is on medical leave. This substitute teacher had not been trained on the district policy. I recommend that this teacher be trained on the policy at the earliest possible date. In addition, I believe that the training of substitute teachers on the district policy is an issue at all district schools. Therefore, I also recommend that the district reexamine the current policy and revise it to ensure that copyright compliance training occurs for substitute teachers throughout the district.

3. The school had documentation that compliance training was occurring. This documentation consisted of a sign-up sheet, kept on file by Mr. Brown, for training attendees. I noticed that the date of the training did not

appear on the sign-up sheet. The training was conducted by Mr. Brown, and he was able to find the date by reviewing his personal calendar. However, I recommend that, in the future, the date of the training appear on the sign-up sheet. Mr. Brown agreed and will include the date for all upcoming training.

4. Mr. Brown has received thorough instruction in copyright law in the past. However, new changes in the law have occurred since his last training. I recommend that he be scheduled for updated training as soon as possible. I will provide Ms. White and Mr. Brown a list of training available locally that will fulfill this need.

Signed _____ Date _____

Rebecca P. Butler
School Library Media Specialist
Thomas Jefferson High School
Copyright Compliance Auditor

Attachment: Completed Audit Checklist

SAMPLE DISTRICT AUDIT PROCESS ANNUAL PLANNING CALENDAR AND LEGEND

Various aspects of a school district's copyright compliance audit process occur over the course of a school year. Shown below is an example of an annual planning calendar that will help ensure that the audit process remains viable on an ongoing basis.

Planning Item	Aug.	Sept.	Oct.	Nov.	Dec.	Jan.	Feb.	Mar.	Apr.	May	June
1. Conduct new employee copyright compliance training.	XXX										
2. Conduct annual copyright compliance training for all.	XXX	XXX									
3. Determine copyright compliance audit schedule.		XXX									
4. Assign auditors to meet the schedule.		XXX									
5. Communicate audit schedule to district office and schools.		XXX									
6. Train new auditors as required.		XXX	XXX								
7. Conduct compliance audits at district office and schools.			XXX	XXX	XXX	XXX	XXX	XXX			
8. Confirm completion of audit recommendations.						XXX	XXX	XXX	XXX		
9. Determine need for additional auditors, if any, for next year.								XXX	XXX		

Figure III.1. Annual Planning Calendar

Annual Planning Calendar Legend

1. Conduct new employee copyright compliance training. This training should occur as part of new employee orientation prior to the beginning of each school year. The training should occur for all new employees throughout the district. In our example, the training takes place in August.

2. Conduct annual copyright compliance training for all employees. The training may be a refresher for those who have taken the training before. Training should be conducted at the district office and individual schools. In our example, it takes place over several weeks in late August and early September.

3. Determine the copyright compliance audit schedule. The district, in conjunction with the schools, must establish an audit schedule for the year. In our example, this schedule creation takes place in early September.

4. Assign auditors to meet the schedule. Using your list of trained auditors, assign individuals to co-conduct the district and school audits for the school year. In our example, this assignment occurs in September.

5. Communicate audit schedule to district office and schools. Once the audit schedule and auditor assignments have been determined, this should be communicated to the district office and the schools so that they have ample time to prepare for the audits. In our example, this communication occurs in late September.

6. Train new auditors as required. If new compliance auditors have been identified for the school they will need to be trained on the audit procedures prior to initiating the audits. In our example, this training occurs from mid-September to mid-October.

7. Conduct compliance audits at the school district office and individual schools. Actual auditing takes place over several months of the school year. During this time, the district office, as well as all individual schools in the district, must be audited. In our example, the auditing occurs from mid-October through March.

8. Confirm completion of audit recommendations. The audits will result in issues and recommendations. It is important to follow up and make sure that the issues are addressed before the end of the school year. This follow-up should occur approximately two months after the completion of individual audits. In our example, this follow-up occurs from January through mid-April of the year following the start of the new employee copyright compliance training.

9. Determine the need for additional auditors for the next year, if any. Over time, the district will need to identify additional auditors. This may be for a variety of reasons: retirement of existing auditors; new schools in the district, requiring a larger auditor pool; etc. The end of the school year is a good time to try to anticipate auditor needs for the following year. In our example, this occurs from mid-March to April.

TOOL IV SELECTED SECTIONS OF THE U.S. COPYRIGHT LAW (TITLE 17 OF THE U.S. CODE)

Tool IV contains selected sections of the U.S. Copyright Law, 1976: Public Law 94-553 (Title 17 of the U.S. Code) of importance to those employed in K–12 education: copyright owner rights; several statutory exemptions: fair use, library reproduction, educational use of works, and duplicating of works for disabled students; provisions of copyright ownership; and limitations on liability relating to material online. For the complete law plus amendments to Title 17 since 1976, see www.copyright.gov/title17/.

106. EXCLUSIVE RIGHTS IN COPYRIGHTED WORKS

Subject to sections 107 through 122, the owner of copyright under this title has the exclusive rights to do and to authorize any of the following:

(1) to reproduce the copyrighted work in copies or phonorecords;
(2) to prepare derivative works based upon the copyrighted work;
(3) to distribute copies or phonorecords of the copyrighted work to the public by sale or other transfer of ownership, or by rental, lease, or lending;
(4) in the case of literary, musical, dramatic, and choreographic works, pantomimes, and motion pictures and other audiovisual works, to perform the copyrighted work publicly;
(5) in the case of literary, musical, dramatic, and choreographic works, pantomimes, and pictorial, graphic, or sculptural works, including the individual images of a motion picture or other audiovisual work, to display the copyrighted work publicly; and
(6) in the case of sound recordings, to perform the copyrighted work publicly by means of a digital audio transmission.

107. LIMITATIONS ON EXCLUSIVE RIGHTS: FAIR USE

Notwithstanding the provisions of sections 106 and 106A, the fair use of a copyrighted work, including such use by reproduction in copies or phonorecords or by any other means specified by that section, for purposes such as criticism, comment, news reporting, teaching (including multiple copies for classroom use), scholarship, or research, is not an infringement of copyright. In determining whether the use made of a work in any particular case is a fair use the factors to be considered shall include—

(1) the purpose and character of the use, including whether such use is of a commercial nature or is for nonprofit educational purposes;
(2) the nature of the copyrighted work;
(3) the amount and substantiality of the portion used in relation to the copyrighted work as a whole; and
(4) the effect of the use upon the potential market for or value of the copyrighted work.

The fact that a work is unpublished shall not itself bar a finding of fair use if such finding is made upon consideration of all the above factors.

108. LIMITATIONS ON EXCLUSIVE RIGHTS: REPRODUCTION BY LIBRARIES AND ARCHIVES

(a) Except as otherwise provided in this title and notwithstanding the provisions of section 106, it is not an infringement of copyright for a library or archives, or any of its employees acting within the scope of their employment, to reproduce no more than one copy or phonorecord of a work, except as provided in subsections (b) and (c), or to distribute such copy or phonorecord, under the conditions specified by this section, if—
  (1) the reproduction or distribution is made without any purpose of direct or indirect commercial advantage;
  (2) the collections of the library or archives are (i) open to the public, or (ii) available not only to researchers affiliated with

the library or archives or with the institution of which it is a part, but also to other persons doing research in a specialized field; and

(3) the reproduction or distribution of the work includes a notice of copyright that appears on the copy or phonorecord that is reproduced under the provisions of this section, or includes a legend stating that the work may be protected by copyright if no such notice can be found on the copy or phonorecord that is reproduced under the provisions of this section.

(b) The rights of reproduction and distribution under this section apply to three copies or phonorecords of an unpublished work duplicated solely for purposes of preservation and security or for deposit for research use in another library or archives of the type described by clause (2) of subsection (a), if—

(1) the copy or phonorecord reproduced is currently in the collections of the library or archives; and

(2) any such copy or phonorecord that is reproduced in digital format is not otherwise distributed in that format and is not made available to the public in that format outside the premises of the library or archives.

(c) The right of reproduction under this section applies to three copies or phonorecords of a published work duplicated solely for the purpose of replacement of a copy or phonorecord that is damaged, deteriorating, lost, or stolen, or if the existing format in which the work is stored has become obsolete, if—

(1) the library or archives has, after a reasonable effort, determined that an unused replacement cannot be obtained at a fair price; and

(2) any such copy or phonorecord that is reproduced in digital format is not made available to the public in that format outside the premises of the library or archives in lawful possession of such copy.

For purposes of this subsection, a format shall be considered obsolete if the machine or device necessary to render perceptible a work stored in that format is no longer manufactured or is no longer reasonably available in the commercial marketplace.

(d) The rights of reproduction and distribution under this section apply to a copy, made from the collection of a library or archives where the user makes his or her request or from that of another library or archives, of no more than one article or other contribution to a copyrighted collection or periodical issue, or to a copy or phonorecord of a small part of any other copyrighted work, if—

(1) the copy or phonorecord becomes the property of the user, and the library or archives has had no notice that the copy or

phonorecord would be used for any purpose other than private study, scholarship, or research; and

(2) the library or archives displays prominently, at the place where orders are accepted, and includes on its order form, a warning of copyright in accordance with requirements that the Register of Copyrights shall prescribe by regulation.

(e) The rights of reproduction and distribution under this section apply to the entire work, or to a substantial part of it, made from the collection of a library or archives where the user makes his or her request or from that of another library or archives, if the library or archives has first determined, on the basis of a reasonable investigation, that a copy or phonorecord of the copyrighted work cannot be obtained at a fair price, if—

(1) the copy or phonorecord becomes the property of the user, and the library or archives has had no notice that the copy or phonorecord would be used for any purpose other than private study, scholarship, or research; and

(2) the library or archives displays prominently, at the place where orders are accepted, and includes on its order form, a warning of copyright in accordance with requirements that the Register of Copyrights shall prescribe by regulation.

(f) Nothing in this section—

(1) shall be construed to impose liability for copyright infringement upon a library or archives or its employees for the unsupervised use of reproducing equipment located on its premises: *Provided*, That such equipment displays a notice that the making of a copy may be subject to the copyright law;

(2) excuses a person who uses such reproducing equipment or who requests a copy or phonorecord under subsection (d) from liability for copyright infringement for any such act, or for any later use of such copy or phonorecord, if it exceeds fair use as provided by section 107;

(3) shall be construed to limit the reproduction and distribution by lending of a limited number of copies and excerpts by a library or archives of an audiovisual news program, subject to clauses (1), (2), and (3) of subsection (a); or

(4) in any way affects the right of fair use as provided by section 107, or any contractual obligations assumed at any time by the library or archives when it obtained a copy or phonorecord of a work in its collections.

(g) The rights of reproduction and distribution under this section extend to the isolated and unrelated reproduction or distribution of a single copy or phonorecord of the same material on separate occasions, but do not extend to cases where the library or archives, or its employee—

(1) is aware or has substantial reason to believe that it is engaging in the related or concerted reproduction or distribution of multiple copies or phonorecords of the same material, whether made on one occasion or over a period of time, and whether intended for aggregate use by one or more individuals or for separate use by the individual members of a group; or

(2) engages in the systematic reproduction or distribution of single or multiple copies or phonorecords of material described in subsection (d): *Provided*, That nothing in this clause prevents a library or archives from participating in interlibrary arrangements that do not have, as their purpose or effect, that the library or archives receiving such copies or phonorecords for distribution does so in such aggregate quantities as to substitute for a subscription to or purchase of such work.

(h) (1) For purposes of this section, during the last 20 years of any term of copyright of a published work, a library or archives, including a nonprofit educational institution that functions as such, may reproduce, distribute, display, or perform in facsimile or digital form a copy or phonorecord of such work, or portions thereof, for purposes of preservation, scholarship, or research, if such library or archives has first determined, on the basis of a reasonable investigation, that none of the conditions set forth in subparagraphs (A), (B), and (C) of paragraph (2) apply.

(2) No reproduction, distribution, display, or performance is authorized under this subsection if—
   (A) the work is subject to normal commercial exploitation;
   (B) a copy or phonorecord of the work can be obtained at a reasonable price; or
   (C) the copyright owner or its agent provides notice pursuant to regulations promulgated by the Register of Copyrights that either of the conditions set forth in subparagraphs (A) and (B) applies.

(3) The exemption provided in this subsection does not apply to any subsequent uses by users other than such library or archives.

(i) The rights of reproduction and distribution under this section do not apply to a musical work, a pictorial, graphic or sculptural work, or a motion picture or other audiovisual work other than an audiovisual work dealing with news, except that no such limitation shall apply with respect to rights granted by subsections (b), (c), and (h), or with respect to pictorial or graphic works published as illustrations, diagrams, or similar adjuncts to works of which copies are reproduced or distributed in accordance with subsections (d) and (e).

110. LIMITATIONS ON EXCLUSIVE RIGHTS: EXEMPTION OF CERTAIN PERFORMANCES AND DISPLAYS

Notwithstanding the provisions of section 106, the following are not infringements of copyright:

(1) performance or display of a work by instructors or pupils in the course of face-to-face teaching activities of a nonprofit educational institution, in a classroom or similar place devoted to instruction, unless, in the case of a motion picture or other audiovisual work, the performance, or the display of individual images, is given by means of a copy that was not lawfully made under this title, and that the person responsible for the performance knew or had reason to believe was not lawfully made;

(2) except with respect to a work produced or marketed primarily for performance or display as part of mediated instructional activities transmitted via digital networks, or a performance or display that is given by means of a copy or phonorecord that is not lawfully made and acquired under this title, and the transmitting government body or accredited nonprofit educational institution knew or had reason to believe was not lawfully made and acquired, the performance of a nondramatic literary or musical work or reasonable and limited portions of any other work, or display of a work in an amount comparable to that which is typically displayed in the course of a live classroom session, by or in the course of a transmission, if—

   (A) the performance or display is made by, at the direction of, or under the actual supervision of an instructor as an integral part of a class session offered as a regular part of the systematic mediated instructional activities of a governmental body or an accredited nonprofit educational institution;

   (B) the performance or display is directly related and of material assistance to the teaching content of the transmission;

   (C) the transmission is made solely for, and, to the extent technologically feasible, the reception of such transmission is limited to—

      (i) students officially enrolled in the course for which the transmission is made; or

      (ii) officers or employees of governmental bodies as a part of their official duties or employment; and

   (D) the transmitting body or institution—

      (i) institutes policies regarding copyright, provides informational materials to faculty, students, and relevant staff members that accurately describe, and promote compliance with, the laws of the United States relating to copyright, and provides notice to students that materials used in connection with the course may be subject to copyright protection; and

(ii) in the case of digital transmissions—

(I) applies technological measures that reasonably prevent—

(aa) retention of the work in accessible form by recipients of the transmission from the transmitting body or institution for longer than the class session; and

(bb) unauthorized further dissemination of the work in accessible form by such recipients to others; and

(II) does not engage in conduct that could reasonably be expected to interfere with technological measures used by copyright owners to prevent such retention or unauthorized further dissemination;

(3) performance of a nondramatic literary or musical work or of a dramatico-musical work of a religious nature, or display of a work, in the course of services at a place of worship or other religious assembly;

(4) performance of a nondramatic literary or musical work otherwise than in a transmission to the public, without any purpose of direct or indirect commercial advantage and without payment of any fee or other compensation for the performance to any of its performers, promoters, or organizers, if—

(A) there is no direct or indirect admission charge; or

(B) the proceeds, after deducting the reasonable costs of producing the performance, are used exclusively for educational, religious, or charitable purposes and not for private financial gain, except where the copyright owner has served notice of objection to the performance under the following conditions:

(i) the notice shall be in writing and signed by the copyright owner or such owner's duly authorized agent; and

(ii) the notice shall be served on the person responsible for the performance at least seven days before the date of the performance, and shall state the reasons for the objection; and

(iii) the notice shall comply, in form, content, and manner of service, with requirements that the Register of Copyrights shall prescribe by regulation;

(5) (A) except as provided in subparagraph (B), communication of a transmission embodying a performance or display of a

work by the public reception of the transmission on a single receiving apparatus of a kind commonly used in private homes, unless—

  (i) a direct charge is made to see or hear the transmission; or

  (ii) the transmission thus received is further transmitted to the public;

(B) communication by an establishment of a transmission or retransmission embodying a performance or display of a non-dramatic musical work intended to be received by the general public, originated by a radio or television broadcast station licensed as such by the Federal Communications Commission, or, if an audiovisual transmission, by a cable system or satellite carrier, if—

  (i) in the case of an establishment other than a food service or drinking establishment, either the establishment in which the communication occurs has less than 2,000 gross square feet of space (excluding space used for customer parking and for no other purpose), or the establishment in which the communication occurs has 2,000 or more gross square feet of space (excluding space used for customer parking and for no other purpose) and—

    (I) if the performance is by audio means only, the performance is communicated by means of a total of not more than 6 loudspeakers, of which not more than 4 loudspeakers are located in any 1 room or adjoining outdoor space; or

    (II) if the performance or display is by audiovisual means, any visual portion of the performance or display is communicated by means of a total of not more than 4 audiovisual devices, of which not more than 1 audiovisual device is located in any 1 room, and no such audiovisual device has a diagonal screen size greater than 55 inches, and any audio portion of the performance or display is communicated by means of a total of not more than 6 loudspeakers, of which not more than 4 loudspeakers are located in any 1 room or adjoining outdoor space;

  (ii) in the case of a food service or drinking establishment, either the establishment in which the communication occurs has less than 3,750 gross square feet of space (excluding space used for customer parking and for no other purpose), or the establishment in which the communication occurs has 3,750 gross square feet of space or more (excluding space used for customer parking and for no other purpose) and—

(I) if the performance is by audio means only, the performance is communicated by means of a total of not more than 6 loudspeakers, of which not more than 4 loudspeakers are located in any 1 room or adjoining outdoor space; or

(II) if the performance or display is by audiovisual means, any visual portion of the performance or display is communicated by means of a total of not more than 4 audiovisual devices, of which not more than 1 audiovisual device is located in any 1 room, and no such audiovisual device has a diagonal screen size greater than 55 inches, and any audio portion of the performance or display is communicated by means of a total of not more than 6 loudspeakers, of which not more than 4 loudspeakers are located in any 1 room or adjoining outdoor space;

(iii) no direct charge is made to see or hear the transmission or retransmission;

(iv) the transmission or retransmission is not further transmitted beyond the establishment where it is received; and

(v) the transmission or retransmission is licensed by the copyright owner of the work so publicly performed or displayed;

(6) performance of a nondramatic musical work by a governmental body or a nonprofit agricultural or horticultural organization, in the course of an annual agricultural or horticultural fair or exhibition conducted by such body or organization; the exemption provided by this clause shall extend to any liability for copyright infringement that would otherwise be imposed on such body or organization, under doctrines of vicarious liability or related infringement, for a performance by a concessionnaire, business establishment, or other person at such fair or exhibition, but shall not excuse any such person from liability for the performance;

(7) performance of a nondramatic musical work by a vending establishment open to the public at large without any direct or indirect admission charge, where the sole purpose of the performance is to promote the retail sale of copies or phonorecords of the work, or of the audiovisual or other devices utilized in such performance, and the performance is not transmitted beyond the place where the establishment is located and is within the immediate area where the sale is occurring;

(8) performance of a nondramatic literary work, by or in the course of a transmission specifically designed for and primarily directed to blind or other handicapped persons who are unable to read normal printed material as a result of their handicap, or deaf or other handicapped persons who are unable to hear the aural signals

accompanying a transmission of visual signals, if the performance is made without any purpose of direct or indirect commercial advantage and its transmission is made through the facilities of: (i) a governmental body; or (ii) a noncommercial educational broadcast station (as defined in section 397 of title 47); or (iii) a radio subcarrier authorization (as defined in 47 CFR 73.293–73.295 and 73.593–73.595); or (iv) a cable system (as defined in section 111 (f));

(9) performance on a single occasion of a dramatic literary work published at least ten years before the date of the performance, by or in the course of a transmission specifically designed for and primarily directed to blind or other handicapped persons who are unable to read normal printed material as a result of their handicap, if the performance is made without any purpose of direct or indirect commercial advantage and its transmission is made through the facilities of a radio subcarrier authorization referred to in clause (8) (iii), *Provided*, That the provisions of this clause shall not be applicable to more than one performance of the same work by the same performers or under the auspices of the same organization;

(10) notwithstanding paragraph (4), the following is not an infringement of copyright: performance of a nondramatic literary or musical work in the course of a social function which is organized and promoted by a nonprofit veterans' organization or a nonprofit fraternal organization to which the general public is not invited, but not including the invitees of the organizations, if the proceeds from the performance, after deducting the reasonable costs of producing the performance, are used exclusively for charitable purposes and not for financial gain. For purposes of this section the social functions of any college or university fraternity or sorority shall not be included unless the social function is held solely to raise funds for a specific charitable purpose; and

(11) the making imperceptible, by or at the direction of a member of a private household, of limited portions of audio or video content of a motion picture, during a performance in or transmitted to that household for private home viewing, from an authorized copy of the motion picture, or the creation or provision of a computer program or other technology that enables such making imperceptible and that is designed and marketed to be used, at the direction of a member of a private household, for such making imperceptible, if no fixed copy of the altered version of the motion picture is created by such computer program or other technology.

The exemptions provided under paragraph (5) shall not be taken into account in any administrative, judicial, or other governmental proceeding to set or adjust the royalties payable to copyright owners for the public performance or display of their works. Royalties payable to copyright owners for any public performance or display of their works other than such performances or displays as are exempted under paragraph (5) shall not be diminished in any respect as a result of such exemption.

In paragraph (2), the term "mediated instructional activities" with respect to the performance or display of a work by digital transmission under this section refers to activities that use such work as an integral part of the class experience, controlled by or under the actual supervision of the instructor and analogous to the type of performance or display that would take place in a live classroom setting. The term does not refer to activities that use, in 1 or more class sessions of a single course, such works as textbooks, course packs, or other material in any media, copies or phonorecords of which are typically purchased or acquired by the students in higher education for their independent use and retention or are typically purchased or acquired for elementary and secondary students for their possession and independent use.

For purposes of paragraph (2), accreditation—

(A) with respect to an institution providing post-secondary education, shall be as determined by a regional or national accrediting agency recognized by the Council on Higher Education Accreditation or the United States Department of Education; and

(B) with respect to an institution providing elementary or secondary education, shall be as recognized by the applicable state certification or licensing procedures.

For purposes of paragraph (2), no governmental body or accredited nonprofit educational institution shall be liable for infringement by reason of the transient or temporary storage of material carried out through the automatic technical process of a digital transmission of the performance or display of that material as authorized under paragraph (2). No such material stored on the system or network controlled or operated by the transmitting body or institution under this paragraph shall be maintained on such system or network in a manner ordinarily accessible to anyone other than anticipated recipients. No such copy shall be maintained on the system or network in a manner ordinarily accessible to such anticipated recipients for a longer period than is reasonably necessary to facilitate the transmissions for which it was made.

For purposes of paragraph (11), the term "making imperceptible" does not include the addition of audio or video content that is performed or displayed over or in place of existing content in a motion picture.

Nothing in paragraph (11) shall be construed to imply further rights under section 106 of this title, or to have any effect on defenses or limitations on rights granted under any other section of this title or under any other paragraph of this section.

121. LIMITATIONS ON EXCLUSIVE RIGHTS: REPRODUCTION FOR BLIND OR OTHER PEOPLE WITH DISABILITIES

(a) Notwithstanding the provisions of section 106, it is not an infringement of copyright for an authorized entity to reproduce or to distribute copies or phonorecords of a previously published, nondramatic literary work if such copies or phonorecords are reproduced or distributed in specialized formats exclusively for use by blind or other persons with disabilities.

(b) (1) Copies or phonorecords to which this section applies shall—

    (A) not be reproduced or distributed in a format other than a specialized format exclusively for use by blind or other persons with disabilities;

    (B) bear a notice that any further reproduction or distribution in a format other than a specialized format is an infringement; and

    (C) include a copyright notice identifying the copyright owner and the date of the original publication.

  (2) The provisions of this subsection shall not apply to standardized, secure, or norm-referenced tests and related testing material, or to computer programs, except the portions thereof that are in conventional human language (including descriptions of pictorial works) and displayed to users in the ordinary course of using the computer programs.

(c) Notwithstanding the provisions of section 106, it is not an infringement of copyright for a publisher of print instructional materials for use in elementary or secondary schools to create and distribute to the National Instructional Materials Access Center copies of the electronic files described in sections 612(a)(23)(C), 613(a)(6), and section 674(e) of the Individuals with Disabilities Education Act that contain the contents of print instructional materials using the National Instructional Material Accessibility Standard (as defined in section 674(e)(3) of that Act), if—

  (1) the inclusion of the contents of such print instructional materials is required by any State educational agency or local educational agency;

  (2) the publisher had the right to publish such print instructional materials in print formats; and

  (3) such copies are used solely for reproduction or distribution of the contents of such print instructional materials in specialized formats.

(d) For purposes of this section, the term—
   (1) "authorized entity" means a nonprofit organization or a governmental agency that has a primary mission to provide specialized services relating to training, education, or adaptive reading or information access needs of blind or other persons with disabilities;
   (2) "blind or other persons with disabilities" means individuals who are eligible or who may qualify in accordance with the Act entitled "An Act to provide books for the adult blind", approved March 3, 1931 (2 U.S.C. 135a; 46 Stat. 1487) to receive books and other publications produced in specialized formats; and
   (3) "print instructional materials" has the meaning given under section 674(e)(3)(C) of the Individuals with Disabilities Education Act; and
   (4) "specialized formats" means—
      (A) braille, audio, or digital text which is exclusively for use by blind or other persons with disabilities; and
      (B) with respect to print instructional materials, includes large print formats when such materials are distributed exclusively for use by blind or other persons with disabilities.

201. OWNERSHIP OF COPYRIGHT

(a) INITIAL OWNERSHIP. Copyright in a work protected under this title vests initially in the author or authors of the work. The authors of a joint work are coowners of copyright in the work.
(b) WORKS MADE FOR HIRE. In the case of a work made for hire, the employer or other person for whom the work was prepared is considered the author for purposes of this title, and, unless the parties have expressly agreed otherwise in a written instrument signed by them, owns all of the rights comprised in the copyright.
(c) CONTRIBUTIONS TO COLLECTIVE WORKS. Copyright in each separate contribution to a collective work is distinct from copyright in the collective work as a whole, and vests initially in the author of the contribution. In the absence of an express transfer of the copyright or of any rights under it, the owner of copyright in the collective work is presumed to have acquired only the privilege of reproducing and distributing the contribution as part of that particular collective work, any revision of that collective work, and any later collective work in the same series.

(d) TRANSFER OF OWNERSHIP.
  (1) The ownership of a copyright may be transferred in whole or in part by any means of conveyance or by operation of law, and may be bequeathed by will or pass as personal property by the applicable laws of intestate succession.
  (2) Any of the exclusive rights comprised in a copyright, including any subdivision of any of the rights specified by section 106, may be transferred as provided by clause (1) and owned separately. The owner of any particular exclusive right is entitled, to the extent of that right, to all of the protection and remedies accorded to the copyright owner by this title.
(e) INVOLUNTARY TRANSFER. When an individual author's ownership of a copyright, or of any of the exclusive rights under a copyright, has not previously been transferred voluntarily by that individual author, no action by any governmental body or other official or organization purporting to seize, expropriate, transfer, or exercise rights of ownership with respect to the copyright, or any of the exclusive rights under a copyright, shall be given effect under this title, except as provided under title 11.

512. LIMITATIONS ON LIABILITY RELATING TO MATERIAL ONLINE

(a) Transitory Digital Network Communications. A service provider shall not be liable for monetary relief, or, except as provided in subsection (j), for injunctive or other equitable relief, for infringement of copyright by reason of the provider's transmitting, routing, or providing connections for, material through a system or network controlled or operated by or for the service provider, or by reason of the intermediate and transient storage of that material in the course of such transmitting, routing, or providing connections, if—
  (1) the transmission of the material was initiated by or at the direction of a person other than the service provider;
  (2) the transmission, routing, provision of connections, or storage is carried out through an automatic technical process without selection of the material by the service provider;
  (3) the service provider does not select the recipients of the material except as an automatic response to the request of another person;
  (4) no copy of the material made by the service provider in the course of such intermediate or transient storage is maintained

on the system or network in a manner ordinarily accessible to anyone other than anticipated recipients, and no such copy is maintained on the system or network in a manner ordinarily accessible to such anticipated recipients for a longer period than is reasonably necessary for the transmission, routing, or provision of connections; and

(5) the material is transmitted through the system or network without modification of its content.

(b) System Caching.

(1) Limitation on liability. A service provider shall not be liable for monetary relief, or, except as provided in subsection (j), for injunctive or other equitable relief, for infringement of copyright by reason of the intermediate and temporary storage of material on a system or network controlled or operated by or for the service provider in a case in which—

(A) the material is made available online by a person other than the service provider;

(B) the material is transmitted from the person described in subparagraph (A) through the system or network to a person other than the person described in subparagraph (A) at the direction of that other person; and

(C) the storage is carried out through an automatic technical process for the purpose of making the material available to users of the system or network who, after the material is transmitted as described in subparagraph (B), request access to the material from the person described in subparagraph (A), if the conditions set forth in paragraph (2) are met.

(2) Conditions. The conditions referred to in paragraph (1) are that—

(A) the material described in paragraph (1) is transmitted to the subsequent users described in paragraph (1)(C) without modification to its content from the manner in which the material was transmitted from the person described in paragraph (1)(A);

(B) the service provider described in paragraph (1) complies with rules concerning the refreshing, reloading, or other updating of the material when specified by the person making the material available online in accordance with a generally accepted industry standard data communications protocol for the system or network through which that person makes the material available, except that this subparagraph applies only if those rules are not used by the person described in paragraph (1)(A) to prevent or unreasonably impair the intermediate storage to which this subsection applies;

(C) the service provider does not interfere with the ability of technology associated with the material to return to the person described in paragraph (1)(A) the information that would have been available to that person if the material had been obtained by the subsequent users described in paragraph (1)(C) directly from that person, except that this subparagraph applies only if that technology—

   (i) does not significantly interfere with the performance of the provider's system or network or with the intermediate storage of the material;

   (ii) is consistent with generally accepted industry standard communications protocols; and

   (iii) does not extract information from the provider's system or network other than the information that would have been available to the person described in paragraph (1)(A) if the subsequent users had gained access to the material directly from that person;

(D) if the person described in paragraph (1)(A) has in effect a condition that a person must meet prior to having access to the material, such as a condition based on payment of a fee or provision of a password or other information, the service provider permits access to the stored material in significant part only to users of its system or network that have met those conditions and only in accordance with those conditions; and

(E) if the person described in paragraph (1)(A) makes that material available online without the authorization of the copyright owner of the material, the service provider responds expeditiously to remove, or disable access to, the material that is claimed to be infringing upon notification of claimed infringement as described in subsection (c)(3), except that this subparagraph applies only if—

   (i) the material has previously been removed from the originating site or access to it has been disabled, or a court has ordered that the material be removed from the originating site or that access to the material on the originating site be disabled; and

   (ii) the party giving the notification includes in the notification a statement confirming that the material has been removed from the originating site or access to it has been disabled or that a court has ordered that the material be removed from the originating site or that access to the material on the originating site be disabled.

(c) Information Residing on Systems or Networks at Direction of Users.

(1) In general. A service provider shall not be liable for monetary relief, or, except as provided in subsection (j), for injunctive or other equitable relief, for infringement of copyright by reason of the storage at the direction of a user of material that resides on a system or network controlled or operated by or for the service provider, if the service provider—

    (A) (i) does not have actual knowledge that the material or an activity using the material on the system or network is infringing;

        (ii) in the absence of such actual knowledge, is not aware of facts or circumstances from which infringing activity is apparent; or

       (iii) upon obtaining such knowledge or awareness, acts expeditiously to remove, or disable access to, the material;

    (B) does not receive a financial benefit directly attributable to the infringing activity, in a case in which the service provider has the right and ability to control such activity; and

    (C) upon notification of claimed infringement as described in paragraph (3), responds expeditiously to remove, or disable access to, the material that is claimed to be infringing or to be the subject of infringing activity.

(2) Designated agent. The limitations on liability established in this subsection apply to a service provider only if the service provider has designated an agent to receive notifications of claimed infringement described in paragraph (3), by making available through its service, including on its website in a location accessible to the public, and by providing to the Copyright Office, substantially the following information:

    (A) The name, address, phone number, and electronic mail address of the agent

    (B) Other contact information which the Register of Copyrights may deem appropriate

The Register of Copyrights shall maintain a current directory of agents available to the public for inspection, including through the Internet, in both electronic and hard copy formats, and may require payment of a fee by service providers to cover the costs of maintaining the directory.

(3) Elements of notification.

    (A) To be effective under this subsection, a notification of claimed infringement must be a written communication provided to the designated agent of a service provider that includes substantially the following:

        (i) A physical or electronic signature of a person authorized to act on behalf of the owner of an exclusive right that is allegedly infringed

(ii) Identification of the copyrighted work claimed to have been infringed, or, if multiple copyrighted works at a single online site are covered by a single notification, a representative list of such works at that site

(iii) Identification of the material that is claimed to be infringing or to be the subject of infringing activity and that is to be removed or access to which is to be disabled, and information reasonably sufficient to permit the service provider to locate the material

(iv) Information reasonably sufficient to permit the service provider to contact the complaining party, such as an address, telephone number, and, if available, an electronic mail address at which the complaining party may be contacted

(v) A statement that the complaining party has a good faith belief that use of the material in the manner complained of is not authorized by the copyright owner, its agent, or the law

(vi) A statement that the information in the notification is accurate, and under penalty of perjury, that the complaining party is authorized to act on behalf of the owner of an exclusive right that is allegedly infringed

(B) (i) Subject to clause (ii), a notification from a copyright owner or from a person authorized to act on behalf of the copyright owner that fails to comply substantially with the provisions of subparagraph (A) shall not be considered under paragraph (1)(A) in determining whether a service provider has actual knowledge or is aware of facts or circumstances from which infringing activity is apparent.

(ii) In a case in which the notification that is provided to the service provider's designated agent fails to comply substantially with all the provisions of subparagraph (A) but substantially complies with clauses (ii), (iii), and (iv) of subparagraph (A), clause (i) of this subparagraph applies only if the service provider promptly attempts to contact the person making the notification or takes other reasonable steps to assist in the receipt of notification that substantially complies with all the provisions of subparagraph (A).

(d) Information Location Tools. A service provider shall not be liable for monetary relief, or, except as provided in subsection (j), for injunctive or other equitable relief, for infringement of copyright by reason of the provider referring or linking users to an online location containing infringing material or infringing activity, by using information location tools, including a directory, index, reference, pointer, or hypertext link, if the service provider—

(1) (A) does not have actual knowledge that the material or activity is infringing;

    (B) in the absence of such actual knowledge, is not aware of facts or circumstances from which infringing activity is apparent; or

    (C) upon obtaining such knowledge or awareness, acts expeditiously to remove, or disable access to, the material;

(2) does not receive a financial benefit directly attributable to the infringing activity, in a case in which the service provider has the right and ability to control such activity; and

(3) upon notification of claimed infringement as described in subsection (c)(3), responds expeditiously to remove, or disable access to, the material that is claimed to be infringing or to be the subject of infringing activity, except that, for purposes of this paragraph, the information described in subsection (c)(3)(A)(iii) shall be identification of the reference or link, to material or activity claimed to be infringing, that is to be removed or access to which is to be disabled, and information reasonably sufficient to permit the service provider to locate that reference or link.

(e) Limitation on Liability of Nonprofit Educational Institutions. (1) When a public or other nonprofit institution of higher education is a service provider, and when a faculty member or graduate student who is an employee of such institution is performing a teaching or research function, for the purposes of subsections (a) and (b) such faculty member or graduate student shall be considered to be a person other than the institution, and for the purposes of subsections (c) and (d) such faculty member's or graduate student's knowledge or awareness of his or her infringing activities shall not be attributed to the institution, i—

    (A) such faculty member's or graduate student's infringing activities do not involve the provision of online access to instructional materials that are or were required or recommended, within the preceding 3-year period, for a course taught at the institution by such faculty member or graduate student;

    (B) the institution has not, within the preceding 3-year period, received more than 2 notifications described in subsection (c)(3) of claimed infringement by such faculty member or graduate student, and such notifications of claimed infringement were not actionable under subsection (f); and

    (C) the institution provides to all users of its system or network informational materials that accurately describe, and promote compliance with, the laws of the United States relating to copyright.

(2) For the purposes of this subsection, the limitations on injunctive relief contained in subsections (j)(2) and (j)(3), but not those in (j)(1), shall apply.

(f) Misrepresentations. Any person who knowingly materially misrepresents under this section—

(1) that material or activity is infringing, or

(2) that material or activity was removed or disabled by mistake or misidentification, shall be liable for any damages, including costs and attorneys' fees, incurred by the alleged infringer, by any copyright owner or copyright owner's authorized licensee, or by a service provider, who is injured by such misrepresentation, as the result of the service provider relying upon such misrepresentation in removing or disabling access to the material or activity claimed to be infringing, or in replacing the removed material or ceasing to disable access to it.

(g) Replacement of Removed or Disabled Material and Limitation on Other Liability.

(1) No liability for taking down generally. Subject to paragraph (2), a service provider shall not be liable to any person for any claim based on the service provider's good faith disabling of access to, or removal of, material or activity claimed to be infringing or based on facts or circumstances from which infringing activity is apparent, regardless of whether the material or activity is ultimately determined to be infringing.

(2) Exception. Paragraph (1) shall not apply with respect to material residing at the direction of a subscriber of the service provider on a system or network controlled or operated by or for the service provider that is removed, or to which access is disabled by the service provider, pursuant to a notice provided under subsection (c)(1)(C), unless the service provider—

(A) takes reasonable steps promptly to notify the subscriber that it has removed or disabled access to the material;

(B) upon receipt of a counter notification described in paragraph (3), promptly provides the person who provided the notification under subsection (c)(1)(C) with a copy of the counter notification, and informs that person that it will replace the removed material or cease disabling access to it in 10 business days; and

(C) replaces the removed material and ceases disabling access to it not less than 10, nor more than 14, business days following receipt of the counter notice, unless its designated agent first receives notice from the person who submitted the notification under subsection (c)(1)(C)

that such person has filed an action seeking a court order to restrain the subscriber from engaging in infringing activity relating to the material on the service provider's system or network.

(3) Contents of counter notification. To be effective under this subsection, a counter notification must be a written communication provided to the service provider's designated agent that includes substantially the following:

(A) A physical or electronic signature of the subscriber

(B) Identification of the material that has been removed or to which access has been disabled and the location at which the material appeared before it was removed or access to it was disabled

(C) A statement under penalty of perjury that the subscriber has a good faith belief that the material was removed or disabled as a result of mistake or misidentification of the material to be removed or disabled

(D) The subscriber's name, address, and telephone number, and a statement that the subscriber consents to the jurisdiction of Federal District Court for the judicial district in which the address is located, or if the subscriber's address is outside of the United States, for any judicial district in which the service provider may be found, and that the subscriber will accept service of process from the person who provided notification under subsection (c)(1)(C) or an agent of such person

(4) Limitation on other liability. A service provider's compliance with paragraph (2) shall not subject the service provider to liability for copyright infringement with respect to the material identified in the notice provided under subsection (c)(1)(C).

(h) Subpoena to Identify Infringer.

(1) Request. A copyright owner or a person authorized to act on the owner's behalf may request the clerk of any United States district court to issue a subpoena to a service provider for identification of an alleged infringer in accordance with this subsection.

(2) Contents of request. The request may be made by filing with the clerk—

(A) a copy of a notification described in subsection (c)(3)(A);

(B) a proposed subpoena; and

(C) a sworn declaration to the effect that the purpose for which the subpoena is sought is to obtain the identity of an alleged infringer and that such information will only be used for the purpose of protecting rights under this title.

(3) Contents of subpoena. The subpoena shall authorize and order the service provider receiving the notification and the sub-

poena to expeditiously disclose to the copyright owner or person authorized by the copyright owner information sufficient to identify the alleged infringer of the material described in the notification to the extent such information is available to the service provider.

(4) Basis for granting subpoena. If the notification filed satisfies the provisions of subsection (c)(3)(A), the proposed subpoena is in proper form, and the accompanying declaration is properly executed, the clerk shall expeditiously issue and sign the proposed subpoena and return it to the requester for delivery to the service provider.

(5) Actions of service provider receiving subpoena. Upon receipt of the issued subpoena, either accompanying or subsequent to the receipt of a notification described in subsection (c)(3)(A), the service provider shall expeditiously disclose to the copyright owner or person authorized by the copyright owner the information required by the subpoena, notwithstanding any other provision of law and regardless of whether the service provider responds to the notification.

(6) Rules applicable to subpoena. Unless otherwise provided by this section or by applicable rules of the court, the procedure for issuance and delivery of the subpoena, and the remedies for noncompliance with the subpoena, shall be governed to the greatest extent practicable by those provisions of the Federal Rules of Civil Procedure governing the issuance, service, and enforcement of a subpoena duces tecum.

(i) Conditions for Eligibility.

(1) Accommodation of technology. The limitations on liability established by this section shall apply to a service provider only if the service provider—

(A) has adopted and reasonably implemented, and informs subscribers and account holders of the service provider's system or network of, a policy that provides for the termination in appropriate circumstances of subscribers and account holders of the service provider's system or network who are repeat infringers; and

(B) accommodates and does not interfere with standard technical measures.

(2) Definition. As used in this subsection, the term "standard technical measures" means technical measures that are used by copyright owners to identify or protect copyrighted works and—

(A) have been developed pursuant to a broad consensus of copyright owners and service providers in an open, fair, voluntary, multi-industry standards process;

(B) are available to any person on reasonable and nondiscriminatory terms; and

(C) do not impose substantial costs on service providers or substantial burdens on their systems or networks.

(j) Injunctions. The following rules shall apply in the case of any application for an injunction under section 502 against a service provider that is not subject to monetary remedies under this section:

(1) Scope of relief.

(A) With respect to conduct other than that which qualifies for the limitation on remedies set forth in subsection (a), the court may grant injunctive relief with respect to a service provider only in one or more of the following forms:

(i) An order restraining the service provider from providing access to infringing material or activity residing at a particular online site on the provider's system or network

(ii) An order restraining the service provider from providing access to a subscriber or account holder of the service provider's system or network who is engaging in infringing activity and is identified in the order, by terminating the accounts of the subscriber or account holder that are specified in the order

(iii) Such other injunctive relief as the court may consider necessary to prevent or restrain infringement of copyrighted material specified in the order of the court at a particular online location, if such relief is the least burdensome to the service provider among the forms of relief comparably effective for that purpose

(B) If the service provider qualifies for the limitation on remedies described in subsection (a), the court may only grant injunctive relief in one or both of the following forms:

(i) An order restraining the service provider from providing access to a subscriber or account holder of the service provider's system or network who is using the provider's service to engage in infringing activity and is identified in the order, by terminating the accounts of the subscriber or account holder that are specified in the order

(ii) An order restraining the service provider from providing access, by taking reasonable steps specified in the order to block access, to a specific, identified, online location outside the United States

(2) Considerations. The court, in considering the relevant criteria for injunctive relief under applicable law, shall consider—

(A) whether such an injunction, either alone or in combination with other such injunctions issued against the same service provider under this subsection, would significantly burden either the provider or the operation of the provider's system or network;

(B) the magnitude of the harm likely to be suffered by the copyright owner in the digital network environment if steps are not taken to prevent or restrain the infringement;

(C) whether implementation of such an injunction would be technically feasible and effective, and would not interfere with access to noninfringing material at other online locations; and

(D) whether other less burdensome and comparably effective means of preventing or restraining access to the infringing material are available.

(3) Notice and ex parte orders. Injunctive relief under this subsection shall be available only after notice to the service provider and an opportunity for the service provider to appear are provided, except for orders ensuring the preservation of evidence or other orders having no material adverse effect on the operation of the service provider's communications network.

(k) Definitions.

(1) Service provider.

(A) As used in subsection (a), the term "service provider" means an entity offering the transmission, routing, or providing of connections for digital online communications, between or among points specified by a user, of material of the user's choosing, without modification to the content of the material as sent or received.

(B) As used in this section, other than subsection (a), the term "service provider" means a provider of online services or network access, or the operator of facilities therefor, and includes an entity described in subparagraph (A).

(2) Monetary relief. As used in this section, the term "monetary relief" means damages, costs, attorneys' fees, and any other form of monetary payment.

(l) Other Defenses Not Affected. The failure of a service provider's conduct to qualify for limitation of liability under this section shall not bear adversely upon the consideration of a defense by the service provider that the service provider's conduct is not infringing under this title or any other defense.

(m) Protection of Privacy. Nothing in this section shall be construed to condition the applicability of subsections (a) through (d) on—

(1) a service provider monitoring its service or affirmatively seeking facts indicating infringing activity, except to the extent consistent with a standard technical measure complying with the provisions of subsection (i); or

(2) a service provider gaining access to, removing, or disabling access to material in cases in which such conduct is prohibited by law.

(n) Construction. Subsections (a), (b), (c), and (d) describe separate and distinct functions for purposes of applying this section. Whether a service provider qualifies for the limitation on liability in any one of those subsections shall be based solely on the criteria in that subsection, and shall not affect a determination of whether that service provider qualifies for the limitations on liability under any other such subsection.

REFERENCE

"Copyright Law of the United States, Chapter 5." 2007. Washington, DC: U.S. Copyright Office. Available http://www.copyright.gov/title17/92 chap5.html#512 (accessed October 15, 2008).

TOOL **V** SCHOOL/SCHOOL DISTRICT COPYRIGHT POLICIES

The annotated Web sites listed here are a representative sampling of some of the many varieties of school copyright policies found on the Internet. Their inclusion does not imply that these policies would work in your district. Every school district has unique issues and requirements that must be addressed as you develop your own policy.

"Copyright Guidelines." 2008. Greenville, SC: Greenville County Schools. Available: www.greenville.k12.sc.us/district/web/policy/ copyrgt.asp (accessed October 15, 2008).

> These guidelines are short and concise, with a focus on computer software and Internet policies.

"Copyright Guidelines, Library Services, Jefferson County Public Schools." n.d. Golden, CO: Jefferson County Public Schools. Available: www.jeffcopublicschools.org/departments/profiles/library_ services.html (accessed October 15, 2008).

> This brief statement stresses that all district employees are to follow copyright law and that those who choose to infringe on someone's copyright will not receive legal protection from said district.

"Copyright Policy." 2003. Indianapolis, IN: Indianapolis Public Schools. Available: www.copyright.ips.k12.in.us/ (accessed October 15, 2008).

> Lengthy and informative, this policy covers the law and guidelines as well as permission and copyright warning information and examples of school copyright questions and answers.

"Copyright Policy." 2005. Medford, WI: Medford Area Public School District. Available: www.medford.k12.wi.us/do/Policies/IIBGC%20 Copyright.pdf (accessed October 15, 2008).

> Two pages in length, this copyright policy states that it follows federal copyright law and the congressional guidelines. It additionally lists a number of instances covering the copying or borrowing of works to which the faculty, staff, and students are to adhere.

"Copyright Policy." 2008. Kapolei, HI: Hawaii Technology Academy. Available: www.k12.com/hta/copyright_policy/ (accessed October 15, 2008).

> This Internet-based copyright policy is part of K12 Inc., a company that provides distance learning to K–12 students.

137

"Indian Prairie Community Unit School District 204 Administrative Procedures." 2004. Aurora, IL: Indian Prairie Community Schools. Available: http://clow.ipsd.org/documents/lmc_manual_revisions/Board_Policy_602_R.pdf (accessed October 15, 2008).

This extensive document focuses, for the most part, on copyright guidelines. There is an inaccuracy on page one; copyright protection is actually for the life of the creator/owner plus 70 years.

"Intellectual Property Policy Statement." 2006. Dubuque, IA: Dubuque Community Schools. Available: www.dubuque.k12.ia.us/intellectual propertypolicy.htm (accessed October 15, 2008).

A one-page online guide for this particular school system, the "Intellectual Property Policy Statement" covers school network use.

"Use of Technology Resources in Instruction." 2008. Kennesaw, GA: Cobb County School District. Available: www.cobb.k12.ga.us/centraloffice/adminrules/I_Rules/Rule%20IJNDB.htm (accessed October 15, 2008).

"Use of Technology Resources in Instruction" deals with the Internet: searching, network security, an acceptable use agreement, etc., in addition to a brief copyright statement.

COPYRIGHT TEACHING AND TRAINING MATERIALS ON THE INTERNET

The annotated Web sites listed here are a representative sampling of copyright teaching and training materials found on the World Wide Web.

American Library Association. 2008. "Copyright Advisory Network." Chicago, IL: American Library Association, Office for Information Technology Policy. Available: www.librarycopyright.net/ (accessed November 28, 2008).

This network from the American Library Association provides resources, blogs, forums, and more to librarians and others interested in copyright.

Aoki, Keith, et al. 2006. *Tales from the Public Domain: Bound by Law*. Available: www.law.duke.edu/cspd/comics/ (accessed November 18, 2008).

A graphic novel for the information age, *Tales from the Public Domain: Bound by Law* follows the exploits of Akiko, the copyright superhero, as she battles evil and learns about copyright law in the process.

Bellingham Public Schools. 2003. "Copyright Permission Letter." Bellingham, WA: Bellingham Public Schools. Available: www .bham.wednet.edu/copyperm.htm (accessed November 28, 2008).

Bellingham Public Schools' Web site has long served as a benchmark as to what should go on a school Internet site. Their "Copyright Permission Letter" was created so that students and teachers who wished to borrow from another's Web site and place it on their own could obtain permission to do so. Remember, if you wish to borrow/copy from an Internet site, it is best to e-mail the owner/creator and ask for permission to use their work.

Brewer, Michael. 2007. "Is It Protected by Copyright?" Digital Slider. Chicago, IL: American Library Association Office for Information Technology Policy. Available: http://librarycopyright.net/digitalslider/ (accessed November 18, 2008).

This interactive Web site treats its users, through a digital "slide rule," to an easy way to figure out whether or not a work is in the public domain.

Copyright Society of the U.S.A. "Copyrightkids.org." United States: Friends of Active Copyright Education. Available: www.copyrightkids.org/ (accessed November 28, 2008).

Created to teach "school-age children the basics of copyright law," this site offers information from registering your own works to common questions and answers to a copyright quiz. There is also a section for educators and parents.

"Getting Permission." 2004. Austin, TX: University of Texas at Austin. Available: www.utsystem.edu/ogc/intellectualproperty/permissn.htm (accessed November 18, 2008).

Part of the University of Texas at Austin Copyright Crash Course, "Getting Permission" informs about permissions and clearance centers, licenses, international copyright, image and news archives, music performance, play rights, contacting owners, and more. Informative and helpful.

Internet School Library Media Center. 2003. "Copyright for Educators." Harrisonburg, VA: James Madison University. Available: http://falcon.jmu.edu/~ramseyil/copy.htm (accessed November 18, 2008).

A meta-site for educators, parents, and students, "Copyright for Educators" sends users to links from the U.S. Copyright Office to the Copyright Clearance Center to the American Library Association.

Morrison, Tammy. n.d. "Copyright and Fair Use Guidelines." Robertsdale, AL: Elsanor School. Available: http://alex.state.al.us/lesson_view.php?id=7595 (accessed November 28, 2008).

Provided by the Alabama Learning Experience (ALEX), this copyright lesson plan for the elementary grades includes an activity and a PowerPoint, and it can be downloaded to your hard drive.

Newsome, Cathy. 1997. "A Teacher's Guide to Fair Use and Copyright." Washington, DC: George Washington University. Available: http://home.earthlink.net/~cnew/research.htm (accessed November 18, 2008).

Focusing on fair use and education, Newsome's Web site is easily navigated.

Virtual University Professional Development Partnership. "Adventures of Cyberbee: Copyright with Cyberbee." 2005. Westerville, OH: Columbus Education Association and Otterbein College. Available: www.cyberbee.com/copyrt.html (accessed November 28, 2008).

With interactive graphics, a copyright lesson, and access to a number of informative copyright Web sites, "Copyright with Cyberbee" is helpful to both teachers and students.

"A Visit to Copyright Bay." 2002. Joliet, IL: University of St. Francis. Available: www.stfrancis.edu/cid/copyrightbay/ (accessed November 18, 2008).

One of many easily maneuvered copyright sites on the Web, "Copyright Bay" presents copyright information in an entertaining manner, through the visuals of a harbor, cove, reef, inlet, etc., all with copyright identities.

Warlick, David. 2003. "Permission Template." Raleigh, NC: Landmarks for Schools. Available: www.landmark-project.com/permission1.php (accessed November 28, 2008).

This is a sample permission template that teachers can use when borrowing from Internet sites for their lesson plans.

Yankovic, Weird Al. 2006. "Don't Download This Video." Available: http://video.aol.com/video/dont-download-this-video/1715468 (accessed November 18, 2008).

For a humorous look at music pirating, access this video and enjoy!

WEB-BASED COPYRIGHT MATERIALS (GENERAL)

The annotated Web sites listed here are a representative sampling of some of the many kinds of copyright information found on the Internet. Please note that some sites take a more conservative approach to copyright law while others "push the envelope." Inclusion of these URLs should not be taken to imply the author's endorsement.

"Acceptable Use Policy." 2008. Austin, TX: Austin Independent School District. Available: www.austinisd.org/inside/technology/aup.phtml (accessed November 28, 2008).

This is an example of a public school acceptable use policy. It also includes a two-sentence statement on copyright and use of the district system(s).

Broache, Anne. 2007. "Backers of Stronger Copyright Laws Form Lobby Group." *ZDNet*. Available: http://news.zdnet.com/2100-9595_22-152143.html (accessed November 28, 2008).

While groups such as Creative Commons promote the loosening of copyright ownership, organizations such as the Recording Industry Association of America, the Association of American Publishers, the Motion Picture Association of America, Microsoft, Viacom and Walt Disney continue to focus on "broad goals like promoting the 'vital role' of copyright in the U.S. economy and job market, encouraging inclusion of copyright protection requirements in international agreements, supporting civil and criminal penalties for piracy, and advocating against 'diminishment' of copyright law." (Broache, 2007: 1).

Chilling Effects. n.d. "Chilling Effects Clearinghouse." United States: Electronic Frontier Foundation and Harvard, Stanford, Berkeley, University of San Francisco, University of Maine, George Washington School of Law, and Santa Clara University School of Law. Available: www.chillingeffects.org/ (accessed November 28, 2008).

Chilling Effects is the joint project of the Electronic Frontier Foundation and several well-known higher education law clinics. The site explains its purpose as:

Chilling Effects aims to help you understand the protections that the First Amendment and intellectual property laws give to your online activities. We are excited about the new opportunities the Internet offers individuals to express their views, parody politicians, celebrate their favorite movie stars, or criticize businesses. But we've noticed that not everyone feels the same way. Anecdotal evidence suggests that some individuals and corporations are using intellectual property and other laws to silence other online users. Chilling Effects encourages respect for intellectual property law, while frowning on its misuse to "chill" legitimate activity. (Chilling Effects, n.d.: 1)

Copyright Clearance Center. 2008. "Copyright Central." Danvers, MA: Copyright Clearance Center. Available: www.copyright.com/ccc/viewPage.do?pageCode=cr10-n (accessed November 28, 2008).

The purpose behind the Copyright Clearance Center (CCC) is to provide users with the information (licenses, permissions, etc.) that they need to borrow or copy others' works. The CCC provides information on copyright and functions as a clearinghouse for a variety of works in a number of organizations.

"Copyright Infringement Notification." 2008. San Bruno, CA: YouTube. Available: www.youtube.com/t/dmca_policy (accessed November 18, 2008).

As this site shows, even YouTube has to deal with the copyright issue. "Copyright Infringement Notification" helps owners who feel that their works have been illegally placed on YouTube go about having their videos removed.

"Copyright and Plagiarism Resources." 2008. Kent, WA: Kent School District. Available: www.kent.k12.wa.us/KSD/it/inst_tech/StudentParentResources/copyright_plagiarism.html (accessed November 18, 2008).

Created by the Kent School District in Kent, Washington, this helpful site pulls together information on copyright and plagiarism from a number of Internet sources. It even explains copyright as found on social networking sites such as Facebook and MySpace.

"Copyright and the Public Domain." 2006. Roswell, GA: Haven Sound. Available: www.pdinfo.com/copyrt.htm (accessed November 18, 2008).

This site helps users find music in the public domain.

"Copyright and Recording Guidelines." 2008. Washington, DC: Cable in the Classroom. Available: www.ciconline.org/copyright (accessed November 18, 2008).

For those who watch and may want to copy from Cable in the Classroom, this set of guidelines is quite informative.

"Copyright Resources for Schools and Libraries." 2008. Madison, WI: Wisconsin Department of Public Instruction. Available: http://dpi.state.wi.us/lbstat/copyres.html (accessed November 18, 2008).

The state of Wisconsin provides the reader with an extensive set of live links for a wide variety of Web sites dealing with copyright law.

Field, Thomas G. Jr. 2008. "Copyright on the Internet." Concord, NH: Franklin Pierce Law Center. Available: www.piercelaw.edu/thomasfield/ipbasics/copyright-on-the-internet.php (accessed November 28, 2008).

This Web page "addresses U.S. copyright issues of concern to those who post to or own email lists or host web pages. It also deals with situations where someone might want to forward or archive another's email posting or to copy material from another's web page" (Field, 2008: 1).

"Free Software, Libre, and Open Source Software (FLOSS)." n.d. United Kingdom: SchoolForge.net. Available: www.schoolforge.net/free-software-open-source-software (accessed November 18, 2008).

This is a link off the main SchoolForge.net site. SchoolForge is a place where "you will find the information, the tools and materials you need to "forge" or make a school and all its parts . . . bringing quality, affordable and dependable software and teaching materials to the people who need them around the world" (SchoolForge, n.d.: 1). The "Free Software, Libre, and Open Source Software" link promotes a type of software license that emphasizes freedom of speech.

Hirtle, Peter B. 2008. "Copyright Term and the Public Domain in the United States 1 January 2008." Ithaca, New York: Cornell Copyright Information Center. Available: www.copyright.cornell.edu/public_domain/ (accessed November 28, 2008).

How to determine whether or not a work is in the public domain is the primary point of this chart. Detailed notes inform the reader.

Hobbs, Renee, et al. 2007. "The Cost of Copyright Confusion for Media Literacy." Washington, DC: Center for Social Media, American University. Available: www.centerforsocialmedia.org/files/pdf/Final_CSM_copyright_report.pdf (accessed November 18, 2008).

In this 17-page report, Hobbs argues for a kinder, gentler copyright law—one that supports media literacy, education, and educators' use of copyright-protected materials in a much looser manner than the mainstream interpretation of the law.

Jassin, Lloyd J. 2004. "Locating Copyright Holders." New York: The Law Offices of Lloyd J. Jassin. Available: www.copylaw.com/new_articles/permission.html (accessed November 28, 2008).

This helpful article outlines how to locate a copyright owner and obtain permission to use a work.

Johnson, Doug, and Carol Simpson. 2005. "Are You the Copy Cop?" *Learning & Leading with Technology* 32, no. 7. Available: www.iste.org/Content/NavigationMenu/Publications/LL/LLIssues/Volume_32_2005_2004_/June_August_Summer_/June-August_2005 .htm (accessed November 28, 2008).

Why copyright infringements occur and how to overcome such occurrences in K–12 schools is the topic of this article.

The Library of Congress. 2007. "H.R. 1201." Washington, DC: The Library of Congress. Available: http://thomas.loc.gov/cgi-bin/bdquery/z?d110:HR01201:@@@D&summ2=m& (accessed November 28, 2008).

At any one time in the U.S. House and Senate, a number of bills are introduced that cover some aspect of copyright law. H.R. 1201 is included here to represent such bills.

Monroe County Community School Corporation. 2007. "Student Access to Networked Information Resources." Bloomington, IN: Monroe County Community School Corporation. Available: www.mccsc.edu/policy.html (accessed November 28, 2008).

The Monroe County Community School Corporation's "Student Access to Networked Information Resources" demonstrates those items often included in a K–12 student acceptable use policy.

"Open Source Audio." 2008. San Francisco, CA: The Internet Archive. Available: www.archive.org/details/opensource_audio (accessed November 28, 2008).

With 187,760 items available for download as of November 28, 2008, Open Source Audio is a site for individuals and groups to both access and donate music. Although sites such as this are sometimes termed "free music sites," in reality, users may be required to abide by Creative Commons licenses placed upon the music by its owners.

Open Source Initiative. 2007. "The Open Source Definition." Available: www.opensource.org/docs/osd (accessed November 28, 2008).

Open Source software is defined.

"PennTags/url/8234." 2005. Philadelphia, PA: University of Pennsylvania. Available: http://tags.library.upenn.edu/url/8234 (accessed November 28, 2008).

Artist Jeff Koons has been named in copyright lawsuits more than once. This Web site summarizes two cases, one in 1988 and the other in 2005. In both instances, Koons infringed on the copyright of photographers during the creation of his art.

"Permissions." 2008. New York: Random House. Available: www.randomhouse.com/about/permissions_form (accessed November 28, 2008).

This is an example of a permission request form from a major publishing company.

Recording Industry Association of America. 2008. Washington, DC: Recording Industry Association of America. Available: www.riaa.com/ (accessed November 18, 2008).

The Recording Industry Association of America (RIAA) has established an extensive Web presence, covering many aspects of the U.S. recording industry. As such, the RIAA "works to protect intellectual property rights worldwide and the First Amendment rights of artists; conducts consumer, industry and technical research; and monitors and reviews state and federal laws, regulations and policies" (RIAA, 2008)

Russell, Carrie. 2006. "Who Owns Your Lesson Plans?" *School Library Journal*. Available: www.schoollibraryjournal.com/index.asp?layout= articlePrint&articleid=CA6302204 (accessed November 18, 2008).

Russell is the American Library Association's copyright specialist. This particular article, found in *School Library Journal*, focuses on answering three educator questions concerning use of PowerPoint slides, PDFs, and lesson plan ownership.

"Sample Permission Letter: Music." 2007. United States: The Copyright Society of the U.S.A. Available: www.copyrightkids.org/letters.html (accessed November 18, 2008).

This is a sample permission letter that might be used when borrowing music from a copyright-protected source.

San Diego County Office of Education. 2008. "Copyright Permission and Release Forms." San Diego, CA: San Diego County Office of Education. Available: www.ivieawards.org/ivie-copyright.asp (accessed November 28, 2008).

The San Diego County Office of Education provides links to sample permission letters and shows where to go to obtain information for copying or borrowing music and movie clips. Helpful and informative.

Simpson, Carol. 2007. "Copyright Incidents Database." Available: www .carolsimpson.com/copyright.htm (accessed November 28, 2008).

Simpson, an author/consultant in ethics, copyright, and school library management, has compiled a database of reported copyright action. While not a complete listing of what copyright infringements, actions, and settlements have taken place in K–12 schools, it is a good place to start when your administrator says, "Can you show me a school that has violated copyright law?"

"Soundzabound: Royalty Free Music for Schools." 2008. Atlanta, GA: Soundzabound Music Library.

Advertised as "the ONLY royalty free music library which meets all the licensing and technology requirements needed for education" (Soundzabound, 2008: 1), it also provides copyright workshops and "FREE downloadable digital music players" to its patrons.

Starr, Linda. 2004. "The Educator's Guide to Copyright and Fair Use." *Education World.* Available: www.education-world.com/a_curr/curr280.shtml (accessed November 18, 2008).

This Web site covers the basics of copyright law for educators.

"Student Acceptable Use Policy Statement." 2000. De Moines, IA: Des Moines Public Schools. Available: www.dmps.k12.ia.us/schooldir/stpolicy.htm (accessed November 18, 2008).

The Des Moines, Iowa, Public Schools Student Acceptable Use Policy Statement directs student use of school networks and the Internet as well as the importance of copyright law and district policy.

Templeton, Brad. 2008. "10 Big Myths About Copyright Explained." Silicon Valley, CA: Brad Templeton. Available: www.templetons.com/brad/copymyths.html (accessed November 28, 2008).

Templeton describes this as an "essay about copyright myths." Originally published in 1998, it was last revised in 2008.

U.S. Copyright Office. 2006. "Circular 22: How to Investigate the Copyright Status of a Work. Washington, DC: U.S. Copyright Office. Available: www.copyright.gov/circs/circ22.html (accessed November 28, 2008).

Circular 22 is a U.S. Copyright Office document that informs users of how to find out whether a work is still under copyright protection.

YouTube. 2008. "Terms of Use." CA: YouTube. Available: www.youtube.com/t/terms (accessed November 28, 2008).

Even YouTube has a copyright policy and terms its users must follow.

INDEX

ABOUT THE AUTHOR

Rebecca P. Butler is a professor in the Educational Technology, Research, and Assessment Department in the College of Education at Northern Illinois University (NIU). At NIU, she teaches graduate (masters and doctoral) classes in school library media and instructional technology. Prior to moving to NIU in 1998, she was an assistant professor in the Department of Curriculum and Instruction at East Tennessee State University (ETSU). While a faculty member at both NIU and ETSU, she has conducted a variety of workshops, conferences, and graduate classes on the topic of copyright. Although the majority has been geared for K–12 teachers and school library media specialists, she has also done numerous presentations on the subject for faculty and staff in various departments at both universities as well as workshops for public, academic, and special librarians. Dr. Butler is the author of *Copyright for Teachers and Librarians* (2004, Neal-Schuman). She also writes a regular column on copyright issues for *Knowledge Quest*, the journal of the American Association of School Librarians (AASL).

Dr. Butler earned a bachelor's degree in library science from the University of Northern Iowa in 1972, a master's of library science degree from the University of Kentucky in 1978, and a doctorate in educational technology/curriculum and instruction from the University of Wisconsin–Madison in 1995. She has worked in a variety of library positions, including several years as a school librarian/library media specialist in public schools (K–12) in Fort Dodge, Dubuque, and Scott County, Iowa, and a private school in Caracas, Venezuela; as a reference and young adult public librarian in Naperville, Illinois; as a medical librarian in Aurora, Illinois; and as a historian/special librarian in Coshocton, Ohio. During her career as a librarian and educator, Dr. Butler has been an active member in a number of professional organizations, including the American Library Association (ALA), the American Association of School Librarians (AASL), the Association for Educational Communications and Technology (AECT), the Illinois School Library Media Association (ISLMA), the Tennessee Library Association (TLA), the American Educational Research Association (AERA), the Freedom to Read Foundation, the International Association of School Librarianship (IASL), the International Visual Literacy Association (IVLA), the Cooperative Children's Book Center (CCBC), and the Wisconsin Educational Media Association (WEMA). In these organizations she has served on a variety of committees, including the Ad Hoc Task Force on Restrictions on Access to Government Information (ALA); the AASL National Conference Evaluation Committee; the AASL/SIRS Intellectual Freedom Award Committee; the Internet, Libraries and the First Amendment Regional Committee (ALA); as an executive board member of the Tennessee Library Association; as co-chair of the (TLA) Intellectual Freedom Committee; and as chair of the History and Archives Committee (AECT). Dr. Butler also worked as a planning committee member of the 2001 Conference on Copyright and Intellectual Property Issues for Online Instruction, Northern Illinois University. Additionally, she served (2006) as a reviewer for the Laura Bush 21st Century Librarian Program. Dr. Butler's research areas focus on copyright, intellectual freedom, and the history of educational technology.